THE **MILLIONAIRE** BUSINESS MINDSET

TABLE OF CONTENTS

CHAPTER 1

VISION AND DECISION

In the 21st century, the word entrepreneur has been thrown around quite a lot. Some people see it as a prestigious title, like a sort of status symbol, while some people see the name entrepreneur as being synonymous to a person who sits at home behind a computer making millions every year. While it is true that there are laptop millionaires who work on extremely lucrative projects from the comfort of their homes while making jaw-dropping amounts of money, entrepreneurship goes beyond that. Being an entrepreneur is more than just a profession or an occupation, it's a way of life. That is why in this piece, I will be describing exactly how to live the entrepreneurial lifestyle; exactly how you can transform yourself and move from where you are in your life right now to the position of a fulfilled, successful business owner who is not only financially stable but can boldly say that they are living the life of their dreams by doing their part to change the world while doing something they are actually passionate about.

There has always been the constant argument over whether entrepreneurs are born or made. The most important quality every entrepreneur must possess is the ability to spot opportunities and viable ideas. These ideas may sprout from their own mind or from someone else's, but the most important thing is that an entrepreneur needs to be able to recognize useful ideas, distinguish them from insignificant ones, and figure out a feasible path to turn that idea from a dream into a commercial success. This ability can be instilled by training and constant practice; therefore, one doesn't need to be born an entrepreneur to offer solutions that can help change the world. You just need to be able to think outside the box and see opportunities where other people can't.

As a soldier in the US army, I served in Korea, Iraq and Afghanistan. All through my stint in the army, I enjoyed serving my country and playing an active, and extremely risky role in serving America, but I always felt like I was cut out for something larger than just serving the army. With every single chance I had, I read business and real estate magazines, articles and media releases. I realized how startup owners all over the world were introducing new creative ideas and innovative solutions to help solve age-long challenges in every sector of the economy from communications to infrastructural development, while making millions of dollars at it. Even right from childhood, I'd always wanted more than just an ordinary life. Serving in the army was a leap in the right direction, but after several years it wasn't providing me the personal satisfaction I desired so much. It didn't take me long to realize that I wanted to become an entrepreneur; own a business that not only generates mind-blowing revenues, but more importantly, play my part in making the world a better place by being the change that I wanted to see in the world.

There were teething problems, quite alright, but I was determined to persevere; more than determined actually, I was desperate. When I left Afghanistan I had no plan, no job to bounce back to, and no network of people. It was honestly like starting from scratch, in this piece therefore, I will be explaining exactly how you can become a successful entrepreneur even if you're starting from nothing.

The first single, most important thing that makes a successful entrepreneur is vision. Having a vision means you have a clear picture of the kind of difference you want to make in the world. Being a visionary sets you apart from the large majority who are just living their lives mechanically day by day, struggling to get out of bed every morning to go to a job that they do not like just to sustain a lifestyle that they hate. Having a vision is not a difficult task, yet a lot of people lack vision. They just cannot visualize exactly what they want to do with their lives, and that is okay. However, in order to become a successful entrepreneur, you need first and foremost, to break out of that vicious everyday groundhog day cycle that keeps you perpetually trapped and renders it almost impossible for you to pursue your dreams. Getting that vision that you would be working towards may not come so easily. Sometimes, you might need to wait a while, and put in some effort into defining your passion and your vision; and exactly how you want to help change the world. In finding your passion and your vision, doing a few things might prove a little helpful.

First of all, you need to be informed. The basis of entrepreneurship is providing goods and services to help fill a void; to solve a problem faced by someone in the world. For your vision to be viable and practicable, it needs to align with reality. Therefore, before you start seeking your passion, it is important for you to understand how important your passion can help contribute to the society at large. Being an avid reader, watching useful, unbiased media releases, and my favorite, traveling the world can help you discover problems that you never knew existed, and in extension, help you discover a way to help solve those problems.

Frequently psychological experts have recommended meditation as a very useful method of helping you to find your passion, and create a vision that you would dedicate your life to. Being informed came before meditation, because having significant, useful information at your fingertips would go a long way in making sure that you think in the direction of the world's most pressing needs, through which you would make the deepest impacts, and in result, generate the largest revenues. Meditating deeply will help you access ideas and make surprising discoveries from the deepest recesses of your mind, thereby enabling you to make the maximum possible use of the most powerful natural asset every human is endowed with. Critical thinking is a skill that the new generation of entrepreneurs needs to master in order to succeed. You need to be able to critically analyze complex situations, make thoughtful deductions, and figure out viable solutions to pressing challenges within the shortest possible period. A vision can be lofty and honorable, but it might not be practicable. Meditating deeply will enable you to think critically about the solutions to be offered to existing problems, and how currently existing solutions can be modified to improve efficiency and speed (a better mousetrap). Discovering a perfect solution to a particular problem that appeals to you while putting factors like cost and practicality into consideration can mean you have found your vision.

While some people try to figure out exactly what they want to do with their lives, they chase perfection, and leave reasonability behind. Chase progress, not perfection. If you chase perfection, you might never settle on a vision, because you will keep thinking of better options rather than settling down to actually begin your journey to entrepreneurship. You need to understand that you might never actually discover the perfect idea, but you will discover an idea that will work. Once you find a workable idea that truly appeals to you, start up on it, and try not to procrastinate. Take immediate and massive action!

While figuring out your vision, it is also important for you to pursue immediate progress, rather than being extremely fixated on the long run. A lot of people never get to start up any of their ideas simply because they do too much of overthinking. It is important for you to plan ahead as much as you can, but it is also inappropriate for you to get so consumed by the future that you never end up getting there at all. Be more concerned about actually beginning, and if you are actually passionate about your vision, you will always find the motivation to forge ahead, persevere and conquer new frontiers with every passing day.

Write down your vision. Writing down what you want to do, probably in the form of a checklist or a must-do list is a very great way of getting things done. To figure out your vision, you need to write down the things that actually set your soul on fire, and then write corresponding problems in the world that can be solved with your abilities and your likes. Getting your ideas in black and white will enable you to achieve an effective kind of objectivity that you may not be able to get if your ideas are only in your head. It will also enable you to have a tangible record of your thoughts as they progress. Therefore, write your ideas, and endeavor to research them to enable you to ascertain how you can finally begin your journey to the life of your dreams.

The next thing to do when it comes to figuring out your vision and ensuring that your dreams come to life is to commit to action. Starting is truly the hardest part of any endeavor. As soon as you find the wherewithal to actually take the first difficult steps towards changing the world, you have passed the most difficult part of your journey to financial freedom and fulfillment. Be committed to actually taking the necessary steps. Remember that if you procrastinate for too long, you will eventually lose the motivation and drive to pursue your dreams, and your dream life might remain just a mirage.

When it comes to bringing your visions to reality, it is also important for you to recognize when to quit. This is a point that is usually not mentioned often enough. A lot of people commit so much energy and resources to ideas that do not work, and eventually they put in so much money and time that when the start-up eventually collapses, they are left with absolutely nothing. It is important for you to be committed to success, however you also need to set some realistic limits for yourself. It might help for you to actually apportion a time limit and cash ceiling for an idea. Within that time frame, pursue that vision with all your might and energy; give it your all. However, know when you have expended enough resources on an idea, and always find the strength Pivot or to move on when appropriate.

Why exactly is it important to have a solid vision before actually embarking on your journey to entrepreneurship?

First of all, starting is hard. It is really difficult to make that decision to risk it all, leave everything behind, and chase a dream. It is however a little more energizing when that dream is a defined concrete vision, an expectation which you hope to achieve within a defined time frame. Being a visionary gives you the drive to begin the tedious journey towards the actualization of your dreams.

Having a definite vision in front of you and in mind also gives you a unique, lethal kind of staying power. No matter how difficult things get, no matter how terrible prevailing conditions are at any point on your journey to success, having a vision will enable you to reflect on your destination in mind, and it will give you the ability to keep defying the odds. If you do not have a concrete vision however, even the slightest challenges would make you begin to reconsider your commitment to your business. Most people make the mistake of jumping into business without actually having a destination they want to arrive at. They just want to make a lot of money, ride the most expensive cars and live in the most luxurious mansions. They do not actually have a defined impact that they want to have on the world. Most people do not even have an idea of how much revenue they want their business to generate. They just want to be entrepreneurs so that they can be rich. People with these kinds of mindsets rarely make it. This is because when the going gets tough, they do not have the vision to encourage them to keep staying on even when everything on Planet Earth seems to be going against them.

Working on a project or running a business that has been an age-long dream can be immensely satisfying, even if financial rewards are not attached. Therefore, when you have a vision; a specific destination that you have had in mind and have been passionate about all your life, then you will discover an incredible amount of satisfaction and contentment when you finally begin to work towards achieving that dream. So, when you begin your journey towards personal financial freedom, even if the big bucks haven't started rolling in yet, the fact that you have finally set yourself on a path towards the achievement of your life-long dreams will give you a feeling of immense satisfaction that will keep you going on even the darkest of days.

Having a vision also helps your business to stand out in a unique, efficient kind of way. Dozens of your competitors are like a significant percentage of most mediocre entrepreneurs out there; they are in business just to make money. They do not have a particular defined impact they want to have on the world. They likely do not even know exactly how much money they want to make, and when they want to make it by. They just want to be rich. You, however, are different. You have a destination in mind, you can picture your vision, and you are fiercely passionate about what you do. You want to change the world, and that inner motivation will drive you to do things with a significant difference. Your dream will spur you to pay more attention to the details that others consider insignificant, and your hard work and consistency which are products of your vision will make you achieve excellence where others fail. I believe in you!

Vision is also extremely essential to the long-term profitability and viability of your start-up. Agreed, there might be a couple of successful businesses whose founders started out with the sole aim to make money without considering the prospect of making an impact on the world, but the fact that you are different, the fact that you are a visionary will make profitability easier for you to achieve. How? When you meditate and try to make a decision about the most practical ways to bring your dreams to reality, you execute a very important step; you match needs and desires with actual solutions. When you properly examine the situation at hand and decide on how you can help offer a lasting solution, you help to make the dreams of thousands of prospective customers come true, and with efficient marketing, your revenues begin shooting through the roof in no time. People who are not visionaries however;

"wantrepreneurs" (want to be an entrepreneurs for the wrong reason) who cannot predict future occurrences based on current happenings, people who do not critically analyze societal needs before starting up businesses, those people barely succeed because they end up being just another face in a fierce and highly populated crowd.

I know you are keen on starting up your business as soon as possible, but it would do you a lot of good to establish a business that would offer a service that you love so much that you would be willing to offer it for free. This particular kind of business would be something you are passionate about, and being extremely successful at it would have been a personal vision for you for years, even if you didn't realize it all along. Executing your vision would enable you to actually change the world with your business, and also allow you to derive an incredible amount of personal satisfaction from being an entrepreneur.

CHAPTER 2

COMING OUT ON THE OTHER SIDE

There are some troubling statistics out there when it comes to people and their money. According to debt.com 19% of all Americans have $0 dollars in access. 31% have less than $500 dollars in the bank. 49% worry about money on a daily basis. 44% could not cover a $400 out-of-pocket expense. Those statistics are alarming. Nearly half of all Americans are just one paycheck away from broke. If you are reading this book and feeling broke, frustrated, or just confused as to how you are going to get out of a financial hole, you are obviously not alone in your struggles. Too many Americans are buying houses they can't afford, buying cars they can't afford, and living lives in general they can't afford. So what advice is out there for those who want to have the millionaire lifestyle?

The most predominant one is Dave Ramsey when it comes to frugality and budgeting. Again, according to debt.com only 32% of Americans actually have a budget. And statistically, you are more likely to have a budget if you make over $75,000. Thusly most people have no idea what they are spending their money on. Dave Ramsey has helped countless people get the financial freedom that they desire through smart budgeting, removing all debt (except mortgage debt), investing in retirement accounts, working with financial advisors and a very simple slow and steady methodology. With this method, you will have an abundance of wealth when you retire. Not getting rich quick with this method is the biggest downside. There is nothing sexy about going slow, methodical, and safe. If you would like to learn more about Dave Ramseys work, he has several books available, but the one I would recommend is, "The Total Money Makeover" by Dave Ramsey. He breaks down the percentages of how much you should save, how much you should invest, and has a very structured outline of what he believes is the best way to help the average American. Dave Ramsey also has a very good podcast which is where you can find a lot of the same information that he uses in his books. Additionally, he has callers explain their financial issues. It is a good way to consume a lot of information in a short amount of time if you don't have time to sit and read his work.

Robert Kiyosaki is the personal recommendation of what it means to have financial freedom. Robert's thoughts on money are based on the modern versions of financial freedom and how most people are given a financial education. How is anyone supposed to make any smart financial decisions if nobody ever taught you how to make money or how to acquire money making assets? The most recommended book to get you into that mindset is "Rich Dad, Poor Dad" by Robert Kiyosaki. The book I would recommend after that is "Cashflow Quadrant". Both of these books are more of a mindset that you need to be in, in order to attract money and what are the best ways in order to accomplish your goals and dreams. Dave Ramsey is more suited for people who want to continue their day job. Robert Kiyosaki is more for those who want to branch out and start their own business. At the very least he will break down how the rich keep their money. What assets pay the least amount in taxes and how you can save more of the money that you have earned.

Grant Cardone is the individual who goes to the extreme when it comes to financial security. Grant Cardone is there for people who want to make millions and who will stop at nothing to accomplish that goal. He isn't opposed to working 100+ hours a week if it means that you gather all of the money that you can. He doesn't promote any kind of work life balance, he doesn't believe in retirement accounts, stocks, bonds or even owning your own home. If you follow his methodology, you do not start any kind of investing until you have at least 100,000 in the bank. Those numbers vary depending on your location, but that is a baseline he likes to promote. In addition, his philology is to only make big moves in the market. You move into a market to dominate that market. This mindset doesn't work for a vast majority of people. His book, "The 10X Rule" is a motivational book that helps explain his mythology. Cardone doesn't have a financial education book like the other previously mentioned authors, but using his mindset, you don't need a financial education breakdown. For Cardone it is an easy formula. If you have debt, you make more money. Do you have a large purchase coming up that you can't afford? Simple, you just make more money. His idea is to make so much money that debt isn't even an issue. Grant Cardone believes there is nothing that you cannot have if your income is great enough.

Each one of these gentlemen has helped shape this book. Having a mix of each one of their best ideas is what I have adopted. The overall hope is that you will continue your financial education and personalize the many financial ideas so that you being to shape your personal approach to money and ultimately your financial vision. Reaching your personal financial goals is such a great feeling. My personal ones in order were, not checking my bank account every time I made a purchase, not paying attention to when payday was, not worrying about if I had the money to pay off my credit card and other bills, automating payments for all of my expenses so I didn't have to think about them any longer and buying whatever I wanted or needed and knowing that I had enough in the bank. There are a few more steps that I am awaiting to accomplish like knowing I can get sick and not go broke, knowing that I no longer need to work, knowing my passive income is going to financially accommodate me for any activities or travel that I want to do, and the ultimate goal is to have money not be an object anymore. While only a fraction of a percent of people have so much abundance that money doesn't matter anymore, that is something worth striving towards. Your goals may be different from my own, but listing them out allows you to create the path towards them. If you are wanting financial freedom, you are going to go down a path that most people are currently not following. You by definition will be doing something that is unique and extraordinary. There will be bumps along the way and a lot of pushback from those surrounding you. The best advice I'm obligated to give is to surround yourself with positive people. Surround yourself with people who are already doing what you are attempting to do. Do not take advice from people who are not doing or have never done what you are trying to accomplish. I see this all of the time. People have given me real estate advice when they don't have any credentials for doing so. I have been given money and business advice from people who are in the 44% who don't have even a small savings of $400 to their name. Regardless of what industry you want to get into, there are always groups of like minded individuals who are doing what you are about to do. Most communities have real estate investing groups, business entrepreneur classes, etc... Research these groups and network with these individuals. Get into the millionaire business mindset and the sky is the limit.

CHAPTER 3

FLEXIBILITY

One of the big sayings that made its rounds in the late 1990's is that you need to do what you love to do. Love what you are doing and you will never work another day in your life. Love what you are doing and you will always find money, happiness and fulfillment. This is an amazingly silly misconception. Every job is stressful including the job that you will love. Every job will overtime burn you out. This is especially true for the entrepreneur. If you are pouring your heart and soul into a business, you are emotionally invested. Thusly you are more than likely to work extended hours, sometimes 80+ hours a week in order to make your dream come true. So what does this mean for you?

You must remain flexible! Flexibility doesn't just mean flexibility for your customers but it also means flexibility for yourself. What makes you as an entrepreneur the happiest? Doing something that you are passionate about, or doing something that makes you a lot of money? If you created a job your passionate about but are not making any money, now you have two issues. Either you are not marketing yourself correctly or the market isn't interested in your product or service. The average individual who is looking to start a business goes through seven iterations of different business ventures before they achieve one that is successful. If you are trying to start a business you must be flexible enough and honest enough with yourself to say that an idea that you potentially have is not a profitable one. By the way, the seven different business ventures is the average before one is successful. It is possible you may go through dozens of business ventures before one sticks. Staying persistence and continuing to move forward is a massive action that most people do not pursue. The market rewards those who take massive action.

If you are not aware of what you are passionate about and you are not aware of what business you are wanting to enter, then you are in an excellent spot to reflect on what problems you have. Identifying a hole in the market that you are able to fill is a good first step into a business. It is an easy correlation to see that if you have an issue with something, then somebody else will have an issue with it as well. The degree of frustration of the issue is a direct correlation of how much potential the business has. As the former owner of Grunts Move Junk, I have seen countless individuals who struggle with an abundance of things that they have collected over the years. The pain point for these individuals is that they felt overwhelmed in their situation. It is incredibly inconvenient to rent a dumpster, throw out all of that stuff by yourself, and then have the dumpster picked up. Not to mention, you only have a limited amount of time with the dumpster. So the customer has to rent this huge dumpster, is on a time crunch, figure out where to throw it, work incredibly hard to toss everything out, and schedule to get it removed. That is an insane amount of work. That is why people decide to hoard everything in their basements. It is much easier to do that than to do all the above-mentioned steps. After hearing about this experience, I recognized the opportunity and combined it with my passion to create jobs for veterans, so I created a junk removal company that employed veterans BOOM! The clients called me, I'd come over with multiple guys, we'd load up all your stuff, take it to the dumpster and the client doesn't have to do or move anything beyond make a phone call and pay a bill. The junk removal service saves the client a ton of hassle and a headache and it filled my internal passion. I would personally pay any organization a ton of money to save me this kind of headache. That is the kind of business you should be striving for; one where it is a win for you, your team and a win for the customer. Something that is easy to understand and brings massive value to the client. If you were to think about the biggest problems that you have right now, I guarantee you there is a business idea somewhere inside your problems.

The other hand, you need to make your services convenient for the customer. This sounds like common sense but think about all of the services that are incredibly hard to utilize because they close at inconvenient times. You need to make sure that your service is known, you are easy to reach, and that you are available when the customer is available. One of the most innovate services trends that I have seen in the last couple of years are the car service industry. I have seen companies willing to travel to an individual's work, clean out their car, wash and wax the exterior, and repair some minor dents. Over the years I found in my business that customers are willing to pay a premium price as long as the value that you provide matches whatever service you are providing. Having a clean car is convenient, couple that with providing more value and individuals are willing to pay more for that service. The banking industry recently started allowing checks to be remotely deposited through their phone application. You no longer need to go to a bank in order to deposit a check. There are services now that allow you to pay a bill with a credit card by swiping your credit card through a card reader or taking a picture of your card and putting it on your phone. Simplifying processes is a huge value. You must create more value in the best manner that you can.

Additionally, there are always tiers of customers in business. There are those that want something for the cheapest price, and then there are the customers that want high-end services. You should cater to each customer base. In continuing to use the car example, every car wash has different levels of service that it provides. There are basic $10 levels where a machine can rinse your car, soap it, spray it with water again, and then dry it off. That is perfect for those customers who want a basic service. Then there are those who are willing to pay the $200 dollar wash, wax, buff, vacuum, rim shine, etc... These customers see the value in their car and $200 is a small amount to pay for them to look presentable in their car. If a car wash only had the $10 option, then you would only be serving those basic tier customers. The higher tiered clients will go somewhere that delivers the value and services that they were looking for. Granted that the high tiered individuals are not a predominant percentage of society, it is still a population that needs to have their needs met. Additionally, there is nothing to say that you cannot upsell the lower tiered individuals. If you have a proven track record of success with the lower paying customers, there is nothing to say that they won't use more of your services in the future and could potentially become a higher paying customer. This is called ascending the value ladder.

Flexibility is the key to displaying value and showing that you have a service that is worthwhile and worth paying for. You will get push back on every aspect of your business and especially pricing. Everyone always wants something for less, or they want something faster, or they want something done in a certain manner. Your pricing is not about the dollar it is all based on value and flexibility. Your business provides extraordinary value and therefor you should never lower your standards or take bad business advice from the individuals that are critiquing you. If they have constructive criticism to add then definitely reflect upon that. Also, take into consensus the feedback that your customers are giving you as far as additional services. I heard repeatedly that construction services should be added to my array of services that I provide. After hearing enough feedback, I added that to my business and it worked out great for a period of time. Then we removed the service when we began expanding across the country. The point is to continue to add value while meeting the customers' needs as best as possible.

CHAPTER 4

HUSTLE

This is the hardest action to practice. Mostly because you can only grind so hard and for so many hours before avoiding burnout. You can only do something for so long before you start to hate it. You can only feel like you are grinding your heals into the dirt for so long and not go anywhere before you give up. Hustling is hard. It requires a form of grit that most people don't have. It requires you to dig deep, become exhausted, make sacrifices, feel like you are lost, and drag you down until you have given everything that you can muster and then it still asks for more. The sad frustrating truth is that somebody is always after your lunch. If you own a business, somebody is always nipping on your heals and is going to try and make something better, more streamlined, or less expensive. There are two modes in business. You are either growing or your business is dying. How do you continue to grow faster, smarter, or make things most cost effective for your customers? How do you make sure that you are on the forefront of everyone's mind when they are selecting a service?

In the beginning of a business, you don't have any choice but to hustle. That just mean's that you have to put in some serious extra hours or be very creative. If you have a family, a social life, or any other obligations outside of your business, you might want to tell them that you are going to be commited and busy over the next few weeks. Get everyone on the same page of your goals. Unless you are superhuman, one of these areas in your life is going to take a hit. It is part of the game. Remember getting started is the hardest part of launching a business. If you are starting from scratch, nobody knows who you are, what you are doing, why they should buy from you. You need to build an audience, and depending on your situation, you might be doing most of the accounting, marketing, scheduling, social marketing, phone calls and emails all by yourself. That is an insane amount of work. In order to accomplish all of this, you need to hustle. Build your million dollar team to support you! You are in this market to dominate. You are trying to make sure that everyone is not able to see any of your competitors whenever they are in need of your services. While I was running Grunts Move Junk, I would spend several thousand dollars a month on online advertisements, I wrote a book promoting my business, I was the top google search result if you queried junk removal anywhere in Vermont. I made sure that I was the first name anyone saw when it came to Junk Removal in Vermont. My team and I constantly made updates to Grunts pages to keep our audience engaged and us in front of them!

Getting back to the point of, once you are established and you have your name out there, and you are starting to get some money, that does that mean that you are finished! You can never coast off of your previous successes. Again if you business is not growing, it is dying. I know several contractors who are very happy going from job to job only on referrals and are very happy living off of those proceeds. They have so much more potential in front of them by building teams to support their success. Success lies beyond yourself it is about lifting others up with you. Once money starts coming into your business, you need to continue the hustle. Add more team members, figure out your weaknesses and hire team members who can do what you struggle with well. You need to keep up that energy. Your hustle needs to be infectious. Your team members need to feed off of your energy, believe in you and your vision, and they will continue to provide the services in the amazing manner that you have. If this is where you are at on this journey and you are looking to build a team. I created a course online at mitchdurfee.com called "How To Build Your Million Dollar Team, and I highly encourage you check it out. It will skyrocket your business success. Once you have begun to grow your team, stay humble and remember that they are doing this for you and with you. Your team is busting their backs because they believe in your vision, your mission, and your business. They are the lifeblood of your company. You cannot grow without dedicated people. Trust me when I say bad morale and unhappy employees are the enemy of the hustle.

Persistence is another key factors when it comes to the hustle. You need to constantly keep pushing in order to get market penetration. If you are wanting a amazing overall market strategy, I would recommend looking up the Ansoff Matrix. There are entire books dedicated to this subject, but the high level overview is as follows. The Ansoff Matrix is a market growth strategy which breaks the idea of marketing and market penetration into four quadrants. Each quadrant dictates which aspect of the market strategy you are wanting to implement.

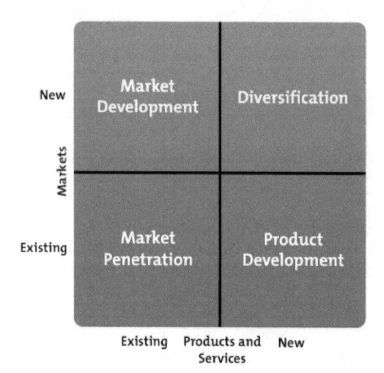

Market Penetration goes into promoting yourself, your brand or your services to new markets or in different manners. With the internet as predominant as it is, you can push your brand to almost a countless number of websites. If you are just getting started, I would recommend sticking with the biggest adverting platforms. For myself, I have found the most success with Facebook and Google. Those two sites along easily hit every group that are in my target market.

Diversification is just as it sounds. You are offering new services that meet your clients needs. The new services should always compliment your primary business. Thus a car repair shop could include car cleaning. A house cleaning business could also turn into a handyman repair business. You need to add products and services that complement what you are already doing. Hiring the right people and anything is possible.

Product Development can be a bit trickier of the marketing strategies. It can be new products or rebranding. Fortune 500 companies are masters at this since they will sell you the same product and treat it like it is a new object. Coke Zero and Diet Coke are virtually the same thing but one was marketed. It is hard to get into specific examples without knowing the integrities of an individual business but think about how rebranding a particular service could help you in getting a different subset of customer engagement.

Finally, there is Market Development. This involves educating the market on your services. The mead business is the first organization that comes to mind. I would like to note that most Americans have no idea mead is an alcoholic beverage that is fermented and sold like wine but has a base of honey and not grapes. If you sold mead you would need to educate your audience and potential customers to what you are offering.

CHAPTER 5

NETWORKING

The most important asset any entrepreneur can have in his cache of skills is his ability to create new, important and functional relationships. It is important for you as a business person to understand your need to expand your professional network, and to actively work on improving your relationship skills. When it comes to the grueling world of business, important connections and relationships can go a long way in deciding the success or failure of your start-up. So, how exactly can you expand your network and create and maintain amazing, functional relationships every day?

First of all, you need to make active efforts, with every passing day to actually show interest in the life of the people you come across. You need to show that you are interested in the lives of your customers, your employees, business partners, and even officials of the regulatory bodies that control the activities of the industry you are working in. Interest is important to creating relationships, so when you meet new people, smile, exchange firm handshakes, and while making small talk, asks useful, targeted questions that show that you are interested in more than just selling your product to the person you are talking with. Show a real interest in the life of the people you come across because everybody is a potential business relationship that could open a new door.

The second and most important part of maintaining your network of relationships within your business circle entails you making active efforts to actually stay in the lives of the important people you met. Most times when we meet people who we think might be beneficial to our future interests, we exchange business cards or phone numbers, and we promise to keep in touch. But how many of us actually make active efforts to remain in touch with the friends we have actually made? Very few! Therefore, as a young, aspiring entrepreneur who is desperate to make a difference using business as their primary tool, you need to be keen about remaining relevant in the lives of friends and acquaintances in the long-term. Remember birthdays, attend hosted functions when you can, reply to e-mails personally, return calls, and once in a while, call to check up on them. All through school, you may not have had a need to periodically scroll through your contacts list and call as much as twenty people in one day, but as a growing entrepreneur, you do. It is therefore extremely important for you to identify the most important and useful connections in the people you meet, and make active efforts to actually remain relevant in their lives.

Why is networking so important to your business? First of all, as I stated earlier, when it comes to business, relationships are everything. You need people, whether you like it or not, and if you need people, it means you need to know how to keep your relationships with them in perfect order. One of the most important reasons why Networking is so essential to the survival of your business is that it helps you to find new business opportunities. When you meet a lot of people, the odds of you stumbling upon a new client or customer who would be interested in purchasing your product or service, or who would even be interested in partnering on a business deal rise. Therefore, networking, meeting new people and maintaining important relationships can help you to actively meet people who can help you take your business to even higher levels!

Apart from helping you to find new customers, networking can help garner invaluable treasures in the form of knowledge and information. The more people you meet, the more you will learn, and the more you are able to stay in those people's lives, the more you will learn still. Important knowledge about new regulatory principles in the industry you operate in, how to get by a particular problem in the business you are engaged in, new, specialized marketing and advertising techniques and a lot more kinds of information can be garnered from the people you meet and maintain cordial relationships with Experienced business partners and friends can also help you get through difficult times in your business.

More experienced key players in the business industry you operate in for instance, might have a reputation with the regulatory bodies and help you avoid getting into trouble with the authorities. Meeting important personalities in your business and staying in touch with them might even help you partner with the big players in the market through programs such as franchises and licensing agreements. With these tools, your business can grow exponentially faster and your dreams of impacting the world will come true sooner than you expect. Bottom line, networking helps you quickly gather quality information from important people in the industry.

Networking can also be essential in helping you source useful advice from experienced professionals and even shrewd customers. As I said earlier, relationships are the pillars of any business, and who could give you better advice on how to improve your business than the people you are actually selling to? To become successful in any genre of business whatsoever, you need to put the opinions of your customers into careful consideration. Hear the views from a personal perspective. Listen objectively to their criticisms and complaints. For a customer to trust you enough to tell you about the shortcomings of your business instead of jumping ship straight away to a competitor, you need to have established a rock-solid relationship with that customer. The problem might not be a huge one. It might just be that you need to negotiate a deal with an office beside you to allow your customers to park their cars with them to avoid getting parking tickets since you do not have enough parking yet. These little things can help contribute to the growth or decline of a business. Therefore, endeavor to listen to your customers, and do not just listen, filter through to the facts and act on the reasonable advice they give you.

Thankfully, with the advent of technological advancements in the 21st century, you can get access and maintain a dedicated online channel for your network. If you are looking for access to a mastermind group of individuals that have a similar goal of growing their business to extraordinary levels visit MitchDurfee.com to join a mastermind retreat or our annual mastermind networking group. The great thing about these dedicated online channels is that you can easily establish contact with other business owners that can give you suggestions, advice, and strategies on your business, and save you thousands! This makes online channels way more efficient than trying to connect in person.

Apart from mastermind business owners network, the second most important people you can source advice from are the experienced key players in your industry. Even if they are your biggest competition, you need to keep your friends close and your competition closer They may have been in the industry before you, they know how the business climate in your region operates, and they know how to get past the tricky situations you might face because they have been there before. They might also have access to more resources to dedicate to research and development, so they might have discovered newer and easier ways of carrying out certain business processes or more efficient methods of handling certain challenges way before you do. Therefore, it is important for you to associate with experience. This will help you to discover newer and more efficient ways of carrying out your business, and might even save you a lot of cost in the long run. Don't get hung up on the thought that they are your competition, There is plenty of business to go around and competitors entering the space will create more market awareness! All you need to do is focus on providing more value and the best experience possible to your customers.

It is also extremely important for you to maintain cordial relationships with every single team member working for (with) you. A lot of business owners see employers as tools to get the work done. If you are going to grow your company into an efficient mechanism that helps to deliver quality products and services at the most competitive rates and with the most excellent customer service, you are going to need to start seeing your employees as more than just resources, and as actual partners in progress. Employees can spell the doom or success of your business. It is your employees that interact with the consumers. It is your employees that actively deliver the service you render. Sometimes, it is even a dedicated employee that handles your company's public relations or the funds that your company realizes. The fact that employees execute such key functions in your organization means that you must maintain the relationship as you would with friends, or else, they can ruin you. Yes, you can fire and sue them for corrupt practices or negligence, but the damage would already have been done. Therefore, with every passing day, make a mental note to, forget yesterday, focus on the future, and interact more with every employee working with you to build your dream life. Talk to them about their work; listen to their feedback and suggestions. They might even have relevant information from the customers they interact with. Tweak your relationships with your employees to the extent that they become integral parts of the company representing its interests everywhere they go. That is how you build a million dollar business. As I always say, "Do more for the people around you, than you would ever expect from them."

Networking also helps in growing your personal profile. When you make active efforts towards meeting new people, and when you try, to the best of your abilities to maintain the relationships you create, you will find out that you will gain a lot more exposure for yourself and more importantly, for your business. To get more exposure, network with complete strangers, you will inevitably inform them about your business. Just like that, you have made a potential client who will definitely think of the warm, smart professional they talked to at a conference some months back when they or someone they know needs a service or product related to your business. Even better, the people you talk to about your business can actually carry out unpaid marketing for you! It is not unusual for people to tell their friends about the people they meet, and when you tell a wide array of people about your business, it makes it easier for your business to gain a wider reach. When you do something nice for someone, those people tell other people, and then those ones tell more people. Next thing you know you're the talk of the town. Your message begins to get much louder as your network becomes your megaphone! The chain will continue to grow, and your company is more likely to experience a growth in sales and partnerships like never before. Therefore, every time you attend an event or talk to a customer personally at your workplace, be sure to ask them if there is anything you can do to help them and ask them to tell others about your business. If you ask nicely, they definitely will. Of course as a networking professional you should also be focused on connecting your contacts with others in your circle of influence!

Networking also helps to improve your self confidence! The more you talk to people, the easier it will become for you to keep talking to people. When you first begin your business as an entrepreneur, you might feel insecure or even petrified about networking. You might be scared that people would not regard you that much or they might even mock your determination to break through in an already saturated market. Allow me to be 100% Transparent, when I first started I met a couple of discouraging personalities, but they do not matter, infact I couldn't tell you their names if they were in the same room as me. Focus on the big picture, the people that matter most are the positive ones who patronize your business when they need your services, encourage you to be better and tell others about your business. As you attend more events and talk to more people, your self-confidence begins to grow. At first, you may not be able to approach the top guns in your industry for advice and help, but as you keep networking, you will find that your self-confidence levels begin to skyrocket, and you would feel more comfortable in your skin even while you are talking to very important personalities. This self-confidence would go a long way in affecting your business and personal life. When people detect confidence and calmness in your approach, they are more likely to listen intently to what you have to say, and your business is likely to get a wider reach. In your personal life too, the self-confidence you gain through networking would boost your self-esteem and help you create new, beautiful personal relationships without the fear of rejection or scorn. By the way, in case nobody has told you recently, you are perfect just the way you are, so there is no reason to be uncomfortable! Networking regularly over a long period of time will lead to you being so confident in your approaches that you are no longer bothered about the outcome of an approach since you have faced so many positive results you will forget completely about those few negative results. Outcome independence will now further help increase your chances of positive encounters because you will be more composed, fluent, and you would display an aura of a incredible self-esteem.

Finally, networking helps you to help others. As you grow your business and attain new heights of professional achievement, you will start to meet people who would look up to you in their personal lives. This is one of the immense joys of being a visionary; knowing that you have actually begun to touch lives. As you keep networking, you will meet people who will need your help. Going out to network and meet new people will bring you in contact with these individuals, and also enable you to render any kind of help possible to enable them move forward. Apart from the warm, fuzzy feeling that helping others brings, helping people can help grow your business. Putting in a good word for someone to help them land a dream job or a promotion will etch your name permanently in that person's mind, and with every opportunity that comes, that person would do all they can to help promote your business in places that you probably didn't even know exist. Therefore, networking will give you the opportunity to give back to the society that helps you grow, thereby enabling you to fulfill one of the key pillars of entrepreneurship – changing the world one person at a time.

CHAPTER 6

SERVING OTHERS

According to Robert Ingersoll, we rise by helping others. Entrepreneurship is not just about creating a product or service and selling it; it is about reaching out and helping to fill an age-long void, playing one's part in helping to make the world a better place. Some of the most experienced entrepreneurs of all time have said the most surefire way to success in business is to make monetary gains a secondary goal. Of course, you might want to make profits and keep your company thriving, of course you might want to go on that dream vacation with your family to a remote island and relax on the beautiful fine sand; of course you might want to buy that sleek Ferrari. However, if you put monetary gains in your business before serving others, your business would likely end up not being exemplary. The best way to establish and maintain a profitable business is to put others first. Whatever you do, make sure that you are attempting to serve others first.

I honestly am still trying to figure out how so many people have not realized that the best way to run a business is to keep in mind that you want to help people; that you want to solve a problem that people have in mind. This mindset will help open your mind to a plethora of opportunities that others cannot seek because they are thinking too selfishly. When you examine these opportunities critically, you will then find ways to monetize your business, and you will end up making huge profits. Let us examine the cases of some of the most successful tech start ups in the world today.

Amazon.com was founded by Jeff Bezos in the 90s on Jeff's home computer. When Bezos started Amazon, the immediate goal wasn't really to make billions. The goal was to enable people to shop for products from the comfort of their homes. Jeff had a vision of a company that allowed people to comfortably purchase products that weren't readily available in their localities without having to travel long distances just to get the things they needed or desired. At first, it seemed like an almost charitable idea. All that Bezos wanted was to establish a viable system that allowed people to buy things. He put the interests of people first. He wanted people to buy things comfortably from the luxury of their homes. He wanted to eradicate the need for people to travel long distances just to buy a couple of essential products. From that idea of wanting to help people, Jeff grew Amazon into one of the world's most profitable companies, and he is currently the world's richest man. He devised means along the way to make profits from his business and grow his company into a multipurpose organization. The key take away is, put others first. Think of how you can serve the society, and I promise you, you will become rich both financially and internally.

Another very brilliantly simple idea that has brought its owner billions of dollars is Facebook. When Mark Zuckerberg established Facebook in his Harvard dorm room in the early 2000s, he likely didn't know he would make such a huge fortune from it. Mark's idea was to create a company that helped people to communicate cheaply over the internet. From that dream to help people, Facebook has evolved over the years to become a multi-billion dollar company and Mark keeps rising, acquiring new companies and implementing new business ideas. From the idea of helping people communicate, additions like Facebook ads have come up to help immensely grow small and medium scale enterprises among so many other developments. The most important thing is for you to be willing to meet a very important need among the people. Work towards meeting this need, and you might have just begun your journey to stardom and incredible wealth.

Why then is it actually important to have the mindset of serving others?

Serving others helps to increase the profitability of your business. When you begin a business with the aid of serving people, you will think primarily of how to meet their needs rather than how you will meet your own needs. When you put others before yourself, it makes you able to see things from their point of view and make reasonable tactical decisions. When you view topical societal issues and needs from the point of view of others, it enables you to come up with a business idea that will efficiently solve the problem in question. This will help you to establish a business that will be hugely patronized, that will grow in leaps and bounds, and will eventually generate millions of dollars in profits. Just do yourself and your business a favor, and think about others rather than yourself.

Helping others also helps you build the most effective relationships and establish viable connections. When you reach out to help others and put their interest before yours, it sends a very powerful message about you and your business. This message will compel people to see you as a different kind of entrepreneur, one who actually puts others first. From this, important business relationships can sprout, and you can make friends who would also help you out in times of need or when you hit a rough patch.

Helping others efficiently helps you give back to the community that raised you. Helping others in this context might mean committing a portion of your yearly revenue to helping needy but intelligent students go to college, or making funds available for small business start-ups. These kinds of gestures would not only help give your corporate image a massive boost, they will help you to create a lasting impact in the lives of people. That is worth more than anything money can buy.

Helping others can also help establish you as an experienced, seasoned expert, and this can encourage people to spread the word about your business. In the entrepreneurial world, relationships are everything. When you take your time to help someone out with a technical problem for instance, it helps the person to see you as an expert at your job, and how brilliant the services you render must be. This will help you to attract a new client for future transactions, and it will even help you garner referrals to your business through that person. Imagine being an experienced mechanical technician running an auto-care workshop. Suddenly on your way home after a long day, you find out that a car has broken down in the middle of the highway, leaving the owner in intense distress. Luckily, you have some necessary tools in your trunk, and you help to fix the person's car. It might even be a problem the person has been managing for a while because other auto-repair shops couldn't repair it. However, you will help make a massive difference by fixing that problem. Instantly, you will make a new, regular client as you tell them about your business, and probabilities are high that that person would tell their friends about the angel-like mechanic that helped fixed their car when they were coming back from work.

How do I know this? Well my first company was a mechanic repair shop, and on my way home from a mastermind meeting, this older lady was driving down the highway and I watched her wheel fall right off her car. It was a rainy day, and the wheel flew across the center median into the other lane of traffic as she swerved back and forth trying to keep her car on the road. Without even thinking I through my hazards on, jumped out of my car, ran across the median and grabbed her wheel and carried it back to her vehicle. I could see she was nearly in shock from what just happened. I jacked up her car, removed one lug nut from the remaining three tires and placed her tire back on her vehicle. I could see in her eyes that she was still in shock from what happened but I believe she was just as much in shock that I went out of my way to help her.

The bottom line is, whatever business it is that you operate, never compromise your relationships, and always remember to do more for others first. It will help your business grow, and trust me; you will derive well over a million-dollars worth of personal satisfaction from it.

The Millionaire Business Mindset

Interview with Mitch Durfee.

Table of Contents:

BACKGROUND

Chris Kelly:

This is The Millionaire Business Mindset with Mitch Durfee and Chris Kelly. I'm interviewing my friend, my colleague, business entrepreneur Mitch Durfee. To get us started Mitch Durfee, tell us a little bit about yourself.

Mitch Durfee:

Well Chris, for as long as I can remember I was always an entrepreneur, and you always hear entrepreneurs say this because there is a vision inside our heads that we don't know how to get out from a really early age. But for myself, when I was in high school I joined the army because I wanted to do more than what I thought was possible for myself, and even when I was overseas I was studying real estate because I was really passionate about making different sources of income even while I was currently working. Not only was I thinking about real estate, but I was also thinking about other businesses that I could start. I just, I've always been passionate about business.

Chris Kelly: Do you feel like the entrepreneurship is something that is innately born inside of somebody, or do you think it's learned? Do you think it's nature? Do you think it's nurture?

Mitch Durfee: That's a great question and I think it's a little bit of two parts. You don't have to be born an entrepreneur to become an entrepreneur, but I think what it is as you grow up, you start to see more opportunities around you, and sometimes your mindset shifts directions towards that. So if you see something that you like, internally your body starts to get attracted to that, and that's just how it's been for me for business. So to answer your question, no. I don't think you need to be born an entrepreneur to become an entrepreneur. I think you just need to see an opportunity and want to do something better.

Chris Kelly: I know that you mentioned that you went into the military. Do you mind expanding on that a little bit?

Mitch Durfee: Yeah. Right out of high school I joined the army. I deployed to Korea, and then I deployed right from Korea to Iraq. I was 19 years old while I was in Iraq. I went to Ramadi, Iraq and I spent a year there. I was mechanized infantry with the 2nd Infantry Division Bravo 5/5, and again, being over there you've have a lot of time to yourself. You're doing a lot of different activities, and a lot of people while I was there, they were reading these Maxim magazines, or car magazines, or fitness magazines. But all I could do was wrap myself around the famous magazines like Entrepreneur, or Inc., or Fortune magazine. It just was something about that, that caught my attention while other people's attention were on other things.

Chris Kelly:

Do you feel like you were an entrepreneur before you went into the army or afterwards?

Mitch Durfee:

That's a great question, and to tell you the truth, I didn't know I was an actual entrepreneur until I was probably 25. I knew I had all these business-driven things, but I didn't realize that was what an entrepreneur was. I don't even know when I actually discovered, "Oh. That's what it is..." When you label it, I didn't know it was actually entrepreneurism. It was business was kind of my thing, just getting more ways to produce ideas that brought me forward more than where I was.

Mitch Durfee:
So it wasn't an income thing, but it was just I knew that I could accomplish more, and that's just why I joined the military, and that's why I started businesses. And then after I think it was probably my third of fourth business that I'm like, "This is actually the part that I really like." After I sold my first business, then the second business. When that started taking off I'm like, "Okay. I like the startup phase. I like the early phases. I don't like the long-term part of it." And that's how I dove into being the "entrepreneur."

Chris Kelly:
I know with the army there are stringent routines. You have to be the most dedicated. You have to be your peak physical form, and by the way, thank you for your service, but how do you feel like the military has helped you in your entrepreneurship?

Mitch Durfee: I think going back to the military, the thing that really sticks out to me is that they had so many different routines. They had systems for everything. Jokingly, we always joked, "I'm sure there's a system, a standard operating procedure for going to the bathroom in the field." And truth is, there probably is something like that somewhere. In business, you don't want to put the red tape up when it comes to your business. Meaning you don't want to block people from their creativity, but what you do find is that if you're able to create systems or routines, there is a shift in your mind that it makes ... I call it decision fatigue. If you have to make less decisions throughout the day, then you're more likely to be successful because the decisions that you do make are more accurate, more on point, and on par with the goals you're actually attempting to achieve.

Chris Kelly: And is that something that you've implemented inside of your business, and if so, what routines do you implement in order to stop that decision fatigue?

Mitch Durfee: Absolutely. If you look at the great franchises like McDonald's you see that they have developed systems. Now, they obviously don't want their employees to be too creative, but they're not successful because their employees are boxed in. They're successful because they have systems in place. Those systems that I look at are systems as simple as uniforms. If you have a uniform for your team members, when they wake up and come into work, well now that is one less decision, and the army taught me that. So to be clear, you want to balance creativity in your businesses because you want that opportunity for them to think outside the box.

Mitch Durfee: But if you're a service business, and you're looking for uniformity, and you're coming to a customer's house, you want your customers to know what to expect. You want your employees to be able to make one less decision, whether that means you start at the same time during the day. Every day you start at 7:00 am, that's a simple thing. If you change it every day, your employees will also shift their routines and they have to make that decision. They have to go change their systems, and when they do that, they're not able to really excel at their best abilities.

Chris Kelly: What is your initial thoughts when I say innovation verse routine. What is the driving factor that causes a successful business?

Mitch Durfee: Well, success can be measured in many ways. Some people find success through fulfilling their passion, and some people find success through fulfilling profits. So, I think that depending on how you fall on that spectrum is really going to decide the fact on whether you need to be more innovative or you need more routines. I think we always hear this buzz on innovation, right? Innovation always cures all, but you'll find that in business, generally 20% of the time those tasks that you're doing 20% of the time are making 80% of your profits.

Mitch Durfee: So, there's no reason to add different flavors of ice cream just so you have more innovation, "Oh, let's combine coconut, and pistachio, and all these different flavors." Because at the end of the day, it's not about the different flavors. It's about what people are actually buying in business. When you find the system that works, you have to get to routines that actually make you more efficient, more streamlined, more directional, and that's what customers are buying. Innovation in the beginning is important, but over time you don't want to reinvent the wheel every day. So, that's when you go to routines when you have those systems in place.

Chris Kelly: To your ice cream analogy, you would say people need to stick with ... If their vanilla is their best seller, they need to figure out how to promote vanilla to its best of the ability?

Mitch Durfee: Absolutely. In business... A lot of business people will recognize this. It's better to go deep than it is to go wide, although in the beginning if you go wide, you cast a wide net, you'll catch a few fish in there. But when you're catching the big fish you have to go deep. So over time, yes. You may want to start off by trying to understand what the customers want, right? That innovation, but after a while you're going to realize that in order to be efficient, what you have to do is focus on what is actually working and start to cross out the projects that you're doing that aren't efficient, that can be better, more profitable, more simple, by creating routines around those processes.

GRUNTS MOVE JUNK

Chris Kelly: Tell me a little bit about how you started Grunts Move Junk.

Mitch Durfee: Yeah. With Grunts Move Junk, I realized that I had a couple different skills. I was in real estate at the time and I was selling a couple houses a month. I just, wasn't really finding my groove in real estate early on, and that's mostly because I didn't have a network. I had just got back from Afghanistan when I got my real estate license thinking that, "Hey. I'm going to fulfill my dreams and I'm going to dive deep into becoming a real estate agent." Well, when you go through your entire phone log and there's only like seven names in there, it's very hard to be a successful real estate agent unless you're door-knocking and you're doing all these other things.

Mitch Durfee: But what I did see was an opportunity for my friends that were also unemployed. They had challenges finding jobs because they were just coming back too. I also noticed there was other agents in the office that were selling houses and I'm

59

like, "Well, these people have to be moving, and my friends need a job, and everyone who was in the military, became really good at moving because we moved every six to eight months." And it just made perfect sense.

Mitch Durfee: I reached out like, "Hey. Listen. If you need a couple of laborers, a couple people that are awesome, you can trust them, they're good people. When they come in your house, you don't have to worry about anything because you're in good hands. If they're good enough to serve our country, they're definitely good enough to serve you." And I'm like, "This business is something that everyone needs, and it's a win/win both ways, right?" The customers wins because they have their problem solved, and the employees and team members win because they have a job that they can look forward to.

Chris Kelly: This was a conversation that I was going to have a little bit later on, but is it important to have every business venture compliment the primary source of your income?

Mitch Durfee: I think the people that find the most success are able to curate vehicles that are on the same highway. So to answer your question, if you're going down the road and you have 10 different directions that vehicles can go into, whether that's real estate, construction, landscaping, those kind of services, it's better to go into those niches and create vehicles that create some kind of synergy inside your business. If you have a real estate business and on the other side you have a moving company, it works well together because you sell the house, and now the next service down is they have to move.

Mitch Durfee: Or for example, if you have a lender in your family and you're a realtor, well you can feed leads back and forth. So, it's much better for your customer value ladder to have services that align in the same industry. That is of course if you're going to open up multiple industries, You don't want to learn how to put a wheelchair together if you're selling houses. They just don't align, The learning curve is much shorter when you're in the same industry.

Chris Kelly: Getting back to Grunts Move Junk, what do you think were some of the pitfalls in order to have it expand across the entire nation, or just some of the pitfalls that you ran into in your first one or two years?

Mitch Durfee: The biggest challenges that a lot of businesses find is always hiring talent and building teams, and that's why I actually created a course that's designed around building a million dollar team. Now, that course is specifically designed to help businesses understand what it is that makes a team successful, and it limits the challenges that teams have, it also streamlines the hiring process. If you have challenges in your business, it's usually because of systems or people. So for pitfalls, if you hired the wrong people, then you're always going to have challenges because the wrong person is always going to be pulling the boat in the wrong direction.

Mitch Durfee: Now, imagine if you have a team of 10 people and six people are on that team and they're pulling one direction, and you have four people that you brought in that were the wrong people or were pulling the boat in the opposite direction. Well, you're going to have a hard time reaching your goals without correcting those people that are pulling in the wrong direction or cutting the rope and releasing them back into the work force. So for pitfalls, I would say the biggest challenge is always building a team that share the same vision as you.

Chris Kelly: How did your processes get better over time when it comes to hiring, when it comes to getting new jobs, new leads, what have you?

Mitch Durfee: We talked about innovation and routine earlier. Now when it comes to processes, I always say if you throw a new process out there, it's likely that it's not going to be instantly successful. It's more likely that it will fail, and that's just being honest. If you put a new process in place, it's more likely that it will fail than it will be successful. So, early on and you're starting a new process in place, the only thing that makes a process smoother is time. If you flip a coin 100 times, it's going to land on heads or tails, right? You know that there's two outcomes, but when you create a process there's many,

many more outcomes than just heads or tails, 50/50, or whatever those statistics actually pay out to be.

Mitch Durfee:

So when you create a system, and you go back to it, and you review the system, I always say the first thing you want to do is you want to write it out with your team because your team has the best insight on how the process. should actually be done, and then you have the vision that actually directs them. Usually they have a few different ideas on how to move the ball forward, but when you're the business entrepreneur you know where the goal is (The Vision). So, you have to work with your team and collaborate with them, and then you have to assign task's to your team and give it a deadline.

Mitch Durfee:

Like, "For 10 days we're going to try this. I know it sounds like a stretch, and I might it sound like it may not work, and it may sound like it is crazy, but in the end, the reason we're doing this is to make your job easier, and more simplified. I think we can both agree that when this works, it's going to put this problem to rest so that we never have to worry about this problem ever again." Over time, you pick out the biggest needles that are just literally bleeding your profits out, and you create systems and processes around those, and over time it all comes together and the whole ship flows much smoother and smoother is faster.

Chris Kelly:

The business strategy and services that Grunts provide is, and correct me if I'm wrong or if I'm missing anything, moving objects, junk removal, basic landscaping. Used to be in construction, but you're no longer in that space. Am I missing anything?

Mitch Durfee:

Yes. When we started Grunts, that was essentially the idea. The long-term vision going back to when I was in the army was to create a business model that padded onto real estate as its core. For as long as I can remember, I always dreamed about buying real estate properties because I knew that. I was focused on starting a business that created more income, so that I could invest in real estate, so that It would pay me dividends forever. Early on when I wrote the idea for grunts it was, "Okay.

65

here's what we're going to do. I'm going to sell them a house, and when I sell them a house, then we're going to have a team move them in. While they're living there and when they're ready to move out, we'll be able to do any kind of repairs that they need,"

Mitch Durfee: So, that was the construction side. We move them in. We did the construction, and when they're getting ready to move again, we had the junk removal side of things, and then we had the ongoing maintenance and landscaping. Now, we looking back we got way too wide early on, and we realized that there was two services that we were really good at, and that was the moving and the junk. After a few years we removed the construction and the landscaping.

Chris Kelly: Does that go back to the 80/20 rule?

Mitch Durfee: Absolutely.

Chris Kelly: In retrospect, you were not making any money on the construction side of your business?

Mitch Durfee:

Absolutely, and early on we believed that the construction was going to be a great resource because, I wanted to flip homes. And that was the idea if I had these teams that could do this, it would make it much easier for us if we had the construction team in-house, and I think that's what you find a lot of developers do. These construction companies that are putting up houses, when they're able to find subcontractors or their own staff that can manage it, that's when you start to make a lot more margins.

Mitch Durfee:

So, we did the same thing with Grunts. We realized that these were different services that we wanted to do. So we started building teams around that, and when we started flipping houses in between other projects it work out really well. Now, again, the challenge is always keeping the big picture in mind and staying focused on that and never getting distracted by the small minor jobs like mowing a yard. Like landscaping, we were more focused on the bigger landscaping jobs, not like a weekly contract service of mowing a yard because it didn't actually add value to the big picture.

Chris Kelly:
In such a physical atmosphere as Grunts, the way you make your money is in volume. So, how did you utilize technology as a business strategy?

Mitch Durfee:
Yeah, Chris. The big thing that you find these days, is that most of the things that we're doing today have already been done, either by someone else at some point in time, and so, we're really just all about optimizing. How we used technology at grunts was we really focused on our website, which is actually the other reason why we started another business, OnlineStartupBox.com we became really good at digital marketing because we were doing it in our business. So, we started building websites for other businesses as one of those business opportunities that we saw we excelled in, and we hired an amazing team to be able to do staff that.

Mitch Durfee:
But to answer your question, technology is really what actually drove that business forward. Everyone was so used to getting an invoice mailed to them in the service business, right? You come out, do the work and you mail the

invoice. Well, we showed up with tablets, and smart phones, and had technology that we could actually do onsite invoicing right there, Job completed, here is the bill. And take the payment right away. So, there wasn't that lag time of collecting the payment down the road. It was instant. It was done, and the customers could go on about their day, and we could move onto the next customers service.

Mitch Durfee: We used that. We also used simple things like GPS, everywhere we went, one of the policies that we put in place was, "Listen. You know you're leaving from point A. Use your GPS to get to point B because even though you know the way, sometimes when there's bad traffic there are alternative routes." And that saved us, I would say, tens of thousands of dollars over time just using a simple GPS.

Chris Kelly: And just in terms of customer satisfaction, I'm sure that were very grateful at the fact that they're able to pay their bill and not have to sign a check, send it out, wait for it to get out of their account, and then on the flip side have you wait for them to sign the check and then have to keep track of everything that's paid and not paid in whatever software you use, and it's just less of a headache all around.

Mitch Durfee: Absolutely. Yeah. Simplify everything. That must be Apple's model, I think, but the truth is the more you do it, the more your customers are going to give you feedback over time on what they want. And pay attention to your customers because people always say that the customers are the number one most important part of a business, and it's partially true, but I believe the truth is your team that you work with is actually number one because if you make your team number one, they're going to make the customers feel like they're number one.

Mitch Durfee: So although your customers are going to give you feedback, you're not going to get that actual feedback back from your customers unless you reach out to them and ask them for that information. So we did, and that was one of the reasons why we were voted as of the best moving companies in the state of Vermont, and

70

we expanded to four different states in a couple years. It was because we simplified our processes and we listened to our customers.

Chris Kelly: And those were a couple of things that you did as far as routines. You always asked for a referral. You always asked to pay electronically. What were some of the others things that you did as far as routines, specifically for Grunts?

Mitch Durfee: Yeah. Going back to automation, we realized that customers love companies with great reviews, so we automated our follow up emails to ask for a review. Also, there are only a few different ways that you can really drive revenue in any business. In fact, there's three ways. It's through more customers. It's through increasing your prices, and it's through referrals. More customers is generating more leads. Increasing your prices, if you add 10% to your product, that's 10% right to the bottom line. And if you add more referrals, for every referral that's basically a new customer, but it grows, and it grows, and it grows.

Mitch Durfee: So, you get one customer and that one customer can turn into six to eight more customers for you. We always asked for those things every single time. How was the service? Can we get the review? And we also frequently upsold. If there was other additional services that we could offer them, while we were there we always offered those services with discounts and promotions to get them to use us again. When we would follow up, we would send a hand written thank you note and in that thank you note it said, "Here's a gift for you or a friend. Let us know how we can help again." And included a promotional coupon. Those little things in general, asking for the referrals, and automating the process is something that really helped us out in the growth of that business.

Chris Kelly: Is there a conversation to be had to where if your business is not growing it's dying because someone else is hungry for your lunch. Someone else is trying to do what you are trying to do. They're trying to do it better, and everybody is always going after the big shark.

Mitch Durfee: Absolutely. I believe the bigger you get in business, the more eyes that come onto you. Early out the gate, you have to literally fill up your bus with rocket fuel in order to get enough momentum so that when people are trying to pull back the leader of the pack, you're so far up front its impossible. They end up planning on how to take you out of the top position instead of focusing on their own business, it really is a great defense. I think it's just human nature, to look up to the top.

Mitch Durfee: If you put two people in the same industry there's going to be a little bit of competition in that business. So you have to innovate in order to get ahead, but again, you also have to create systems so that you don't have to look back. Although, of course when I say that, my first thought is you should always be reviewing what worked in the past, but none the less, create systems. That way you don't have to recreate the wheel every single day, and be in the mindset that if you're partying, someone else is planning.

Chris Kelly: Is technology needed for every single business today?

Mitch Durfee: That's a great question. I think it really depends on the industry. Out West they're doing so many different things like they have these giant tractors that they can push a GPS and it will mow the field automatically. Then of course you have Tesla, it is an amazing car. It can literally drive itself. Tech simplifies things. That feature is something everyone will always adapt to even if they don't want it, everyone's going to want in the future. So if you're not using technology to simplify, then people are going to naturally choose the other business over time because they can offer more value. It's not about technology. It's about value to your customer. You can provide more value through the use of technology, and I think that's why it's important and critical for you to implement technology in any business that you're in.

Chris Kelly: From a personal standpoint, I do not see the mom-and-pop person who only has zero to one employee actually being safe. Some people who are plumbers, who are electricians, go at it single-handedly. They're okay with having one or two referrals making $50,000 to $150,000 a year and just carving out their own little niche section in the market. Do you see that as success or security? Do they need to expand? Do they need to utilize technology?

Mitch Durfee: To answer the question, if I was a small mom-and-pop shop, one to maybe four employees and that's where I currently was, I'd only really have two options. I think over time I would have to grow and adapt the use of tech or I would slowly disappear. I think that's just how it happens in business. If you own a coffee shop and it's just one or two people, and another coffee shop parks right next door to you, and they have a full team, and they have the systems and technology in place, you will still get residual customers because they will like that small homeliness environment. However, unfortunately, the truth is it's much better to implement the technologies so that your business can prosper so that you don't have to worry about the shop next door directly competing

Mitch Durfee: Again, going back to that millionaire team. If you're struggling and you have that one to four employees, then ultimately getting to maybe five, or 10, or 20, or putting systems in place so that those team members, can operate without you so that you can focus on the big picture and get your mindset around the million dollar business that you deserve to be running is the only way to stay ahead of other competition because over time, within five years, someone will come in. They'll have a better website. They'll have the faster car. They'll have the better technology. They'll have better systems. Customers will love them more because they're doing more, providing more value to their customers through technology.

Chris Kelly: And just to elaborate on that point, I know a good number of restaurants whose entire customer base are 60-year-old plus people, and that's how they make their money. And that's how they're able to stay comfortable is these repeat customers, but they're not going to be around forever. And once they slowly stop wanting to spend so much money going out, your business is going to slowly fall apart.

Mitch Durfee: Absolutely. I agree, you are seeing that, especially in the restaurant industry, right? If you went into a restaurant 10 years ago, they never had the tablet where they flip the tablet over and they say, "Okay. Here it is. We'll take your credit card payment right here at the table." You're seeing that implemented because in order for them to serve more customers get you out of that restaurant so they can fill that seat again. In order to streamline that system, they still have to be able to make you feel like you're not rushed but shorten the gap between, "Okay. Let me go way over here in this corner, and stand behind two other employees, and chit-chat at the register. Then come back to you and give you the bill and change, and then walk off and serve another table."

Mitch Durfee: They're able to shorten the steps that they walk during the day which allows them to get more customers in, and more customers that have a better experience at that restaurant. If you're able to serve 30 to 50, or let's just say three times more customers than the other restaurant, you will have three times the revenue, and you'll be able to add more value. when you add more value you'll have customer satisfaction. Those customers will give you more referrals and more repeat business. Resulting in even more revenue. So create those systems... Of course, it really depends on how big you want to grow your business, I'd rather be more worried about how I'm going to serve all these new customers versus why are there no customers. I call these quality problems. So get big, and then get efficient.

OTHER BUISNESSES

Chris Kelly:

Let's now go into some of your other ventures. Tell me a little bit about Green Rock Investments.

Mitch Durfee:

Green Rock Investments. A couple years ago, almost six years ago I realized that as I was reading all these books I needed to figure out how I was going to be able to take companies and sell companies without really affecting the sales, and the 1031s, and just doing all that kinds of paperwork. So Green Rock Investments was created in order for me to, essentially down the road, offer shares to all these other businesses that I intend to hold. Now over the years, Green Rock Investments has held probably eight to 10 different LLCs and DBAs.

Mitch Durfee:

Just start a business. Test it. If it doesn't work, get rid of it kind of thing. Or start a business. Test it. Run with it. If it works, grow it and then sell it. For example, Green Rock Investments actually was the official owner of Grunts Move Junk LLC. So the LLC was held by Green Rock Investments, which was the S Corp, and again there are also some tax benefits to having an S Corp. That was the idea behind Green Rock Investments.

Chris Kelly: What about Online Startup Box?

Mitch Durfee: Online Startup Box was, again, as an entrepreneur what you realize is when you have a problem you have two things, right? You complain about the problem or you create a solution, and Grunts Move Junk early on about a year into the business, we realized that we needed a better website. So, we hired a company because we were already moving pretty fast So we said, "We'll just hire a web design company." And I'm sure a lot of people out there in the world, or they are a the small business, They've dabbled with these Wix sites. They've dabbled with creating their DIY websites. Or they have hired what I call a bad carpenter, right?

Mitch Durfee: You hire a bad carpenter and now you never want to hire another carpenter again. Well, that was my experience. We were growing Grunts, and Grunts was growing really fast, and then we hired a really bad web designer. The site was already generating leads and we thought by going back, and rebuilding it, and making it better it would provide more leads. If we doubled down on the website, it would double down the customers.

Mitch Durfee: So, we hired this company out in Colorado. I won't say their name, but they tanked it. They would take our ad budget, and they would spend it, and there were typos all throughout the website. We were targeting customers in Vermont and the website had spelling errors... The ads even spelled Vermont wrong. The phone number was the wrong phone number on the website. The contact form didn't even have an email address attached to it. It wasn't forwarding the emails when people actually did it, so we would get complaints from customers.

Mitch Durfee: Every time we called them; they're like, "Oh. We'll fix it. We'll fix it. We're on it right now." We were paying them for SEO work. We were paying them for pay-per-click work. We were paying for web design and landing pages, and it got to the point where we literally actually almost shut Grunts down... I had to pull my field manager in, and I pulled my office manager in, and I pulled my marketing manager in, and we all sat down and I said, "What do you want to do? Do you want to shut it down or do you want to keep going with it?"

Mitch Durfee: We all agreed to move forward, "All right. Well listen, if we're going to do this, then first thing we have to do is fire this marketing company." So, we did. We sent off an email firing them, and stayed up all night rebuilding the entire website. After we did, it nothing but growth, after growth, after growth, and we recognized a new opportunity, "Why do we need to hire a company to do this if we are the ones that are actually doing the work?

Mitch Durfee: So what did we do? We built an in-house marketing team, and that in-house marketing team started to create some outstanding work, we realized that we had some resources and tools that were way ahead of anything in the area. We began offering our services to other businesses, and it helped them grow and helped us learn a few more things.

Mitch Durfee: We basically started building websites to help others, and then we actually split that off of Grunts completely and started a whole new company called Online Startup Box, - building websites, and pay-per-click ads, and lead funnels, and marketing strategies, and just consulting businesses on how to get more customers. Again, it solved the pain problem that a lot of people had, right? You hire a bad carpenter, you're worried about hiring another one. But just because you hired a bad carpenter doesn't mean they're all bad.

Chris Kelly: How about becoming an author?

Mitch Durfee: Oh, man. Becoming an author was something that I never thought I would ever do, and that's actually why I did it. It was on the opposite side of my comfort level for me. Going back to high school, my junior year of high school, I failed English. When I failed English it crushed me because I always wanted to do more in my life so failing was hard for me. I always viewed myself as an overachiever, and I had this drive and determination to do big things. When I failed, I literally thought I was going to have to stay back another year in high school, and that made me feel so sick. Now, I did have to retake my english course my senior year, which was fine. What bothered me the most was that, I failed by only .4. I had a 59.6, right? You always remember the number when there's pain there. So 59.6, and me being a math lover I was like, "Okay, fine, round up and give me a D." Unfortunately the teacher wouldn't do that for me. Then I asked if there was any extra credit I could do, still nothing. I was so upset I just gave up on reading! I don't think I read a full book from 2002 all the way through 2012. Finally I cracked, I picked up an amazing book, Think And Grow Rich by Napoleon Hill. When I finished reading it, I fell so in love with reading I regretted all that missed time. Now I read one, sometimes up to three books a week and I almost always carry two books with me everywhere I go.

Mitch Durfee: Did I mention how much I love reading! There's so much knowledge packed into the pages of a book, I realized that if I'm consuming all this knowledge from other successful entrepreneurs. I felt obligated to share the strategies that helped me achieve all the amazing things I've accomplished over the years. I wrote the book Serve 2 Win based on those exact principles. It actually became a number one bestseller in the first 12 hours. My vision was to help others by creating a fulfilled lifestyle through helping others.

Mitch Durfee: If you don't read many books or haven't invested in personal development before the strategies inside of Serve 2 Win puts everything into perspective. These are the eight things that I discovered that helped me grow my businesses and other businesses I coach around the country.

Chris Kelly: I know that you initially talked about becoming a realtor and how that was the first thing that you started doing after you got back from the army. Tell us a little bit more about what made you initially want to take that first step into becoming a realtor.

Mitch Durfee: I was a little naïve at the time because when I was reading these books about real estate and I always saw next to the investors namers was the title real estate agent or broker. They were buying houses, flipping houses, and then selling houses. They would always put their sign with their face on it out front. I felt like, "Okay, well if I ever want to become a real estate investor, then I need to get into becoming a realtor." I studied for the test. It took about six weeks to pass the exam.

Mitch Durfee: I started making the cold calls and knocking on the doors to sell houses. Again, to this day I am still very passionate about getting out there and helping people locate their first home or sell their home. I still love that, but what I personally am fulfilled by is actually doing the investment side, the real estate developments, the fixes and flips, and the buy and holds rentals. These are things that actually drive me internally, but on the otherside, I love helping people, I love educating buyers and sellers about their properties. I combined the too of these and started a facebook group called Real Estate Property

Warriors where the group assists other members with their real estate education journey and their investment journey.

Chris Kelly:

Do you mind elaborating on being a real estate investor, particularly on the point of how it would help Green Rock Investments, Grunts Move Junk, OnlineStartupbox, any of those other services that you provide?

Mitch Durfee:

Early on, when I decided that I was going to get into real estate investing, there's a formula out there. It's very common yet undisclosed formula. You have general partners, and you have limited liability partners. A good friend of mine, Robert Bloch from champlain college shared this concept with me when I would meet with him in between classes. The concept is, the house keeps 10%. Usually as a management fee, or in other words a "deal maker" Fee. You're paying out people to do the work, the general contractors, and materials everything else like that. Then you pay the investors at the end of the day, the company that brings everything together usually keeps a portion of it. Often they don't actually

Mitch Durfee:

use their own money to bring a deal together. When I was reading these books and learning from Mr. Bloch I was discovering the models, I realized that Green Rock Investments would be the parent company that would buy the LLC. They would use the funds of other investors and create income and wealth for those people. Overtime, Green Rock Investments would grow financially and find more partners. Then Green Rock Investments would have more equity so we would be able to buy more properties. The concept was Green Rock would feed our real estate team, our Grunts Move Junk business and our construction business. We would buy a house that needed work. We'd hire our internal crews to do, the demo, the renovations and the fixes. Then after that, we would decide to either sell it and roll the profits into the next property or rent the house out and keep it for our own portfolio.

Mitch Durfee:

There were a couple other businesses we started I don't know if you're familiar with, but I also started a property management company. That again was, one of those things that fell into those similiar categories. Having my own property management company was something that I needed in order to manage the properties. The mindset that is very important is when it comes to starting branch off businesses make sure you are diving deep.

Mitch Durfee: Now the same thing in business. If you have this giant vision that you want to create something like Green Rock Investments, if Green Rock Investments is going to own real estate, then what I did was I drew out five different LLCs that that owned, and I drew out the little box for Grunts Move Junk being one box, and OnlineStartupbox was our web development company. Then I had a question mark in the other one. Below that, I wrote, "How far will we go?" It was just the mindset. We knew what the vision was, and we knew when we accomplished those things on the board we would find the next thing.

Mitch Durfee: Again, going back to when you have that vision. Vision, having a vision is critical even if you have no idea how you will get there! You have to believe it and once you speak it to the world and tell everyone that you're going to do it,. Then if you believe it, then you can achieve it. I always tell people this, every time I achieve a goal, I remember I always go back to the memory that I had when I said it. In January, when I decided to write the book, I knew that by July, I would have that book in my hand. July 1st, 2017 was the day that I was going to have it. When I actually got the book in the mail and I opened up the envelope, I knew exactly what that was going to look like, and feel like. I could picture it vividly

Mitch Durfee: When I received the mail, I knew exactly where I would be, in my dining room, standing by the table "Here it is." I knew the feeling I would get. It's almost like the vision is what actually makes things come true. You just have to trust the process.

Chris Kelly: The latest venture that you're starting to explore is becoming a stock investor.

Mitch Durfee: I've invested in stocks a couple different times when I was in Afghanistan and I had a lot of time to read. When I was over there, I did a lot of options trading and stocks. Again, I try not to give too much advice in this because I'm not a financial advisor yet, but for me, on the stocks, it was a way for me to put money and park it and make a better return than what banks were giving me. I read the magazines, and I studied, and I read the books and followed Warren Buffett and looked to the best mentors in the business.

Mitch Durfee: I just followed what they were doing. By following what they were doing, I was able to come up with my own system, it generates some okay dividends every year. Really, again, the stock investing is just a place to hold the money until I'm able to purchase more real estate or another business.

Chris Kelly: I'm seeing nine different ventures that you've gone on. That's quite the accomplishment, and I noticed that all of them complement each other in the same manner that we were still talking about. Do you agree?

Mitch Durfee: What you're seeing are the businesses that have been successful are the ones that complement each other. What you're not seeing are probably the other

25 businesses that I've started that I ran for three to six months that didn't compliment these industries that actually failed. I think it's very important to note that yes, when you have a business that complements other businesses, they do actually work hand in hand.

Mitch Durfee:

If I didn't have all the other industries already running, it's likely that I would've been able to drive the new ventures to success by using the same strategies as always, help others, have a vision, and relentless progress. Unfortunately, because I was distracted, I was chasing two different rabbits, it didn't actually work out. Yes, I would lean towards if you're getting into business and you want to dive deep, create industries that work together.

Chris Kelly:

You touched on one of my favorite sayings in business, which is fail often and fail fast. I wanted to see if you wanted to elaborate on your thoughts on the matter.

Mitch Durfee:

That is such a great saying. I remember the first time I actually heard someone say this. It was Adam Hergenrother, a very amazingly intelligent and talented entrepreneur. He goes, "fail forward." At the time I never understood exactly what it meant. In fact I thought he said "fall forward" My mind wouldn't allow me to hear it at first, "Fail, why would I want to fail? I want to be successful I don't want the struggles." The truth is in business, you are going to fail, and you're going to fail often. You're will have hard times, but I always say persevere, make relentless progress, you only really failed if you quit. Because here's the thing, if you're creating this amazing beautiful thing, it's very unlikely that you're going to hit it on the first swing.

Mitch Durfee:

As you swing more often, more frequently, and you get corrections and guidance from coaches, mentors and your peers, you're going to be able to perfect that system so well that you just have no other way but success. I always love to tell the story about two bakers. There are two bakers, both bakers are given one week to make the best pie. One reads all the books and reads all the recipe and makes only one "perfect pie". Meanwhile, another baker, says, "I'll make as many pies as I can in the next week and pick one.

Mitch Durfee:
At the end of the week, they each choose one pie, and bring them to the judge. Do you know who won? At the end of the week, the baker that made more pies made the better pie because he created so many different options in that same time period. Now it's the same kind of thing in business and success. Sometimes you learn a thousand different ways not to make a pie, but in then end all you need to do is make one really, really good pie.

Chris Kelly:
Statistically, the numbers differ from study to study, but usually it takes seven to 10 businesses to fail before you actually make one that succeeds. Fail often and fail fast is don't stick with one idea if it's going to do nothing but drag you down and take all of your attention from your other, more potentially successful ideas.

Mitch Durfee:
That is exactly it. Sometimes there's a balance between seeing it through to the other side and knowing when to quit. If you lose the vision, you lose the passion,

if you realize that it's not going to be successful, then you have to drop it. That's what I've done on a lot of these businesses that failed to be profitable or I couldn't see the vehicle or that business -- I call it a vehicle -- being successful in the next six to 12 months, and it wasn't something that I wanted to be married to.

ENTREPRENEUR MINDSET

Chris Kelly: Now let's get into the general millionaire business mindset. Distance yourself away from all of the different projects that you've done successfully, and let's say that you are starting from scratch. With the knowledge that you know, how do you get started?

Mitch Durfee: I think the bigger challenges as you move forward is after you've paid so much tuition in mistakes, it becomes harder to actually get started because you don't want to fail any mores, right. Some say, "Go after what you're passionate about," but I don't completely believe that because if you're passionate about it and you're losing money every day, well there's a bad recipe. You can be passionate and broke. I think there's something to be said about being passionate and broke versus passionate and profitable.

Mitch Durfee: It does have to have some passion because otherwise you're going to give up, quit, leave it. You're going to move onto something different. It also has to be profitable now, or has to fulfill your needs for fulfilling a nonprofit business. For the sake of a million dollar business mindset, it has to be profitable. Now in order for it to be profitable, it has to solve a big problem for people. If you're solving problems, it's not about making money. It's about the solution because the longer that you are in business, you realize that people don't just pay for a product. They're paying for a solution to a problem that they may have.

Mitch Durfee:

For example, people don't go out to Walmart and purchase a vacuum because they say, "Hey, you know what? Today I want a vacuum. I can't wait to have this." The problem that they're trying to solve is the dirt that's on the floor inside their house. The vacuum is a product that solves a problem. In business, when you hear people complaining, you have to open up your mindset to listen to the complaint and be able to offer a solution and realize that people are often willing to pay to have their problems solved.

Chris Kelly: One of the individuals that both of us really respect is Grant Cardone. If you have a millionaire mindset, what are the business strategies and the business strategies that you need to implement in order to potentially be that successful?

Mitch Durfee: As Grant Cardone?

Chris Kelly: Not as Grant Cardone, but if you have a mom-and-pop shop and you want to reach that million dollar and beyond level. Do you need a business strategy to get to a 30 person staffed restaurant? Basically, the 10X logic that Grant Cardone talks about in his book.

Mitch Durfee: One strategy that millionaire business owners have to understand is that there is no chance ... I don't want to say "no" actually, although it is very unlikely. You have to understand that in order to get further faster, the million dollar business and beyond, is it's very difficult to do it on your own. You have to understand that you only have so many hours in a day. In order for you to 10x your income, you have to understand that the precious asset of time is going to be one of the most valuable resource in your business. I'm talking about your time, and the time of others.

Mitch Durfee:

If you are charging $10 an hour and you work or ten hours, that's only $100. It's very difficult to make a million dollars in a year if you can only do that. You can't work enough hours at $10 an hour in a day to earn $1,000,000 in a year. You have to be able to bring in about $3000 dollars a day. Relax though, there is a better way to take the weight of your shoulders. Build yourself a team to help you reach your goals. Now, you have to understand in order to build a million dollar team, your team has to share the same vision with you, the same passions, the same purpose, and you have to present them with opportunities that are going to allow them to also join you on this journey.

Chris Kelly:

One of the most common questions when someone's trying to start a business is that they don't have any money. How do you get started when you have a lack of resources?

Mitch Durfee:

I think it's very important to mention that when I first started, I also didn't

99

have any money, or any network. However I did have the idea, and the resourcefulness to begin. There are some businesses that do have seed capital injected, and they're able to build these huge businesses a little faster. I didn't have that opportunity, even though I tried. I didn't start with a nest egg. I started from scratch. I went out, and I opened two credit cards. If you're starting with no money, you have to figure out a way to be resourceful and provide opportunities that allows you to leverage other people's resources and time.

Mitch Durfee: Stay working the job you're doing now and put a few extra hours in. That is the best time to come up with your strategy or system for the next part of your life, or again, go out and get other peoples money to support your mission. Now it's not a matter of resources. It's a matter of resourcefulness, especially when it comes to real estate investing and businesses in general. If you go up to someone that has money with an amazing idea and it's actually going to make money, then you will be very hard to find someone that won't beg you to let them give you.

Mitch Durfee: That's the business cycle, and people are doing this everyday. There are so many people in this world with amazing idea's but no money. Then there are people in this world with no more idea's, or no free time, but they do have money. Take money that they have, and combine it with someone else's idea and time to create a million dollar business. If you have a million dollar idea, or if you find a property that has an incredible opportunity to make money, bring it to an investor, and they will help you achieve your dreams while simultaneously achieving theirs.

Chris Kelly: What are your opinions on people who go to a job day in and day out, they hate it, but then they're slowly gathering those resources in order to piecemeal their business together?

Mitch Durfee: I'd say move faster! Gather the resources or reach out to a mentor. I also believe it goes back to the chasing two rabbits, right. If you're working at a job and you're earning money on the side business but you haven't quit because you're scared to leap, the only thing you have to do is take action. If you're only able to put two hours to the business a day and it's making (X) dollars, wait for it to balance out. Meaning if you are making the same amount of money or more working for yourself those two hours as you are working for someone else, then just burn the ship and take the island. It's the only way to move forward. My first book book Serve 2 Win explains the importance of taking massive action. The hardest part is getting started if they are working two jobs. They have already started, now its time to be dedicated to their vision.

Mitch Durfee: Identify your vision internally. Speak it to the world. Close your eyes, and take a deep breath. Take that initial leap. Once you get the ship sailing, you'll never dream of going back to working for someone else again. You will never have to either as long as you keep persevering and you follow the strategies in front of you. Remember to reward yourself for your efforts, and your challenges, over time, you will realize it is hard, but it is worth it.

Chris Kelly: One of the things you keep touching on is accountability and how you are not going to be successful if you are not accountable to somebody.

Mitch Durfee: Accountability is a two-way street. You have to be accountable to the people that you lead, and they have to be accountable to yourself. Imagine you're the leader, you have to have someone watching over you and making sure that you're doing the right things. I like to call that my own personal board of directors. For example, one system that helped my businesses grow rapidly and become successful was creating a mastermind group. The mastermind behind our mastermind group was Jay Cummings. Every week, Thursday at 1:00, we meet. We'd sit down, and go around the table, "What's going on with your business this week?" celebrating the successes, uncovering the challenges and focusing on the opportunities in front of each other.

Mitch Durfee: We have a personal board of directors that are able to fine tweak our businesses models and provide massive amounts of value to each other. Each one of us is accountable to each other. The board of directors (mastermind) that we have in G19, is a no kitten glove group. It is more like, "I'm going to tell you the hard things you need to hear in order to make sure you are successful." For example, when I didn't want to finish first my book and I was one month and one chapter away from being done, they were the ones saying, "Not a chance Mitch, you said you were going to do it. Now it's time to get back to writing." Thanks to them, when I was stuck they helped me over the hill. If you haven't had the privilege to experience a higher level of accountability, higher a coach, or invest in a mastermind group. From time to time at MitchDurfee.com I have a few openings for one-one business coaching and access to our annual mastermind group. If you're commited to your business, I challenge you to take action and join a limited exclusive group of serious business players worldwide. The mastermind provides the unprecedented opportunity to network with and learn from myself and other extraordinary business owners.

Chris Kelly: Just because I know you personally, I know that you've posted on your social media, "I'm going to get X dollars in real estate by X date or else I'm donating a certain amount of money to a certain charity." I've seen online to where people write their boss, "I'm going to quit my job one year from today." Do you recommend something like that because initially, it is scary for someone who has not gone through that path?

Mitch Durfee: YES! That's what we call the Ulysses contract. We have to tie ourself to the mast with no turning back so that we can actually get the results our soul wants. When we're talking about that X number in real estate by X date, it was a stretch goal for me. I literally wrote that on the mirror, and saved it a few other places. I not only promised that I would write a check to a business that I didn't I physically wrote the check out signed the check and dated it. I gave it to a mastermind group member Alan Kinney and told him to mail it for me if I didn't contact him by November 19th 2016! Talk about motivation for an entrepreneur to keep driving forward. Writing the goal on the mirror, and actually one of the big things that I love to do is, I like to put my biggest goal on the back of my phone. #goalonaphone.

Mitch Durfee:

The reason putting it on my phone works so well is every time I wake up, I look at my phone, if I want to sleep in or snooze, I have to swipe past my goal. When, I swipe to open my phone, I'm reminded of my goal and then whatever task I'm doing, it has to be goal oriented. If I open up social media, (I'm a big sucker for posting selfies. If you see me out get a selfie with me!) My social media time has to be focused time. Having the goal on my phone really is to hold me more accountable. Accountability just helps pull you forward, If I tell you that I'm going to climb to the of a mountain, and you're standing there watching me do it. Now I have to do it!

Mitch Durfee:

Business owners have to constantly be the ones creating a future vision with their teams. When I say "Hey everyone, I'm going to achieve _____." Now, I have leverage. I don't want to let my team down, and I definitely don't want to let myself down. When I begin the journey there will be some that come with and

106

others waiting at the bottom of the mountain. They want me to get to the top of the mountain safely, before they commit to the climb. That is the reason I am constantly raising the bar and tying myself to the mast. I set this big, scary, crazy goal, it is not easy, but it inspires others, remember on the other side of comfort, is where you start to discover more fulfillment both financially and spiritually. You even find more happiness and more joy.

Mitch Durfee: I just started doing these comfort challenges. Sometimes people will challenge me to go do things, and sometimes they're dumb. Sometimes they're like, "Go up to that person and introduce yourself" or "Go lay down in middle of the airport," or whatever it is. I'll do it just because it is scary. When I first started speaking in public, it was something that really scared me! I never really thought I could do it. In fact, when I took public speaking in college, I would write down every single word on the note card.

Mitch Durfee: I would pretend like I wasn't reading it, but the whole time, I was just reading off

107

the card. My heart was racing the room felt so tiny and I had difficulties getting a full breath of air. The thing most people know deep down but often forget is, things get much easier the more frequently you do them. It is a simple as riding a bike, the first time you crash, you get up and do it again. The reason that I committed to becoming a better speaker is because I knew that I was able to inspire thousands of people and share even more value with the world. It was my obligation to share the strategies, resources and stories with the world.

Chris Kelly:

What is the ultimate goal of an entrepreneur? I know one of the conversations you and I have on occasion is the freedom that having your own business, setting your own schedule brings and the joy of actually building something from the ground up brings because eventually, your business becomes you. You are the face of it. Everything that the business does reflects what is perceived in the community. Grunts did an incredible job as far as doing a ton of charity work and being a good community service leader.

Mitch Durfee: To answer your question, as an entrepreneur, I think the reason we venture down the road is because maybe it's a little bit like at the casino. If we spin the wheel and it lands on red, and you lose a couple hundred bucks, you don't want to give up just yet. You already lost the time that you put in. You lost a little bit of money. You spin the wheel again. Now you're up $50. You spin the roulette wheel again, and you lose a couple bucks. The difference in this example is the house always wins over time. However in business if you persevere and are relentless,you always get the desired results. The only people that don't are the ones that quit to soon.

Mitch Durfee: Continuing to spin the wheel, and yes, it's hard. Sometimes you have to ride that line of not making a dime, but the next week, it's the home run you needed. Maybe its the physiological change we that we're thriving for, the dopamine rush. That's why we stay in that office late at night, and we are up early, we're working towards total freedom. Like being on a perfect life long vacation that you can bring all your friends and family with. Who knows it could get boring after 10 years, but when you're on vacation and you're in that moment, that opportunity is something that most can relate to, no stress, and serenely joyful. They don't want to have to go back to work. They don't want to have to worry about bills.

Mitch Durfee: They don't want to have to worry about paying the doctor to look at a scratch because it might be infected. They don't ever want to have to worry. I believe that the comforting though of an entrepreneur, is we're able to provide that comfort for other people around us. When we're successful, we bring as many other people with us. By doing that and lifting those people up, they're able to do the same thing for more. Before you know it it creates this massive, massive movement.

Chris Kelly: In general, what is the best piece of advice you have ever received in regards to business?

Mitch Durfee: The best advice that I've ever received in business would be go to a coach or a mentor. When you first start off playing a sport or trying anything new, even if you are just starting to get the principles down, you are able to shorten that path by hiring someone, and by learning off someone else's tuition. Use their actual knowledge from them making the mistake's so you don't have to remake the mistakes on your own. I would say that's going to streamline your business every single time. In fact, with Grunts, I knew the direction that I wanted to take it in, and Jay Cummins, had a business years ago that was incredibly successful.

Mitch Durfee: He's been a great mentor to me because anytime I had a challenge, it's almost like, "Oh, to be expected. Here's what I did. I'm not telling you what to do, but here's my experience. Here's how I did it, and here's what worked for me. This may or may not work for you. If you want to give it a shot, it's all yours."

Chris Kelly: Just to elaborate on your point, the best piece of advice I've ever received is don't take advice from people who have not already done what you're trying to do. That leads into the next question of opinions are a dime a dozen. What's the worst piece of advice you've ever received?

111

The Millionaire's Mindset

Mitch Durfee:

Oh wow, I've had some bad advice over the years. Dare I say for me, the worst advice that I've received unfortunately was go to college. That's just me speaking for myself because I spent nine years working towards a bachelor degree that I never actually received. I stopped three classes shy because I started my own business, and it got to a point that my businesses was making me more money than I would be able to make by having a degree and working for someone else. Now every month or so, I do regret that, that I never finished. I'm sure that someday, I will go out and finish my courses.

Mitch Durfee:

For me, it was not the right vehicle for me. The amount of money and time that I invested in college, I should've invested with someone that had experience because if I worked with the best businessperson or the best stock trader or the best real estate broker. Even if I just took the same time that I was in college and paid someone as a mentor, it would've gave me 10 times the knowledge, one to one. It would've shortened the path, and it would've taught me things that I actually needed to know for the industries that I needed. I'm mostly sour to college because I had to keep retaking course as I move in and out of the country with the army. On top of that, there were courses I wanted to take (graphic design, video creation, entrepreneurship) but they weren't apart of my "degree selection." Is there a need for colleges yes, was there a need for me possibly, would I go back and change paths, yes.

Chris Kelly:

If current Mitch Durfee could talk to past Mitch Durfee, what advice would you give to five years ago Mitch Durfee?

Mitch Durfee:

I would say the best advice that I could give to myself is that don't let other people's action affect your emotions and reactions. Now what that means is every single week you will come across people that are either upset about something that you have no control over. Don't let that impact your life. At the same time, when you find someone that inspires you, latch on to them, provide as much value to them, and stay in contact with them even if they don't reply!

Chris Kelly: One of the things that everybody idolizes is the entrepreneur successes, and nobody really talks about some of the hardships that you face in order to get to that point.

Mitch Durfee: Now, I love this question because I think that it's important to share the hardships of being an entrepreneur. I partially believe we don't share the hardships because we are so wired to focus on the good things that happen instead of reminding ourselves of the challenges. In the last five years of being in business, there were countless times that I would come home, and I'd think to myself, "I didn't move my financial needle at all today. In fact, I think it actually went backward." Those days when stacked up, they become very hard, and you start to question, "Should I move forward? Should I continue to do this? Should I pivot? Should I give up? Should I quit?"

Mitch Durfee: Those challenges are only a mental game. If you let them, they will beat you up, and they will hold you back from where you want to be. Be relentless and push forward. The best thing is, instead of focusing on what is wrong, you can focus on the amazing things that are happening around you. When you know what it is that you want to achieve, like helping one person today, your mindset will release all the garbage, and it'll focus on the wins, which of course is ten times better of a feeling than it is when your mind starts to focus on the losses.

Mitch Durfee: Now, our mind only does what we train it to do. Imagine you're walking down the road, it starts to rain and you're upset about it raining. Being upset doesn't solve the problem and it trains our brain to be upset. However if you're walking down the road and you have an umbrella, you're not upset about the rain. Instead you're thinking about the rain watering the flowers. Now that's what business is like and having that business mindset, you have to look for the good things inside of the challenges. You also have to plan ahead for the challenges. Having a positive mindset, and a core support group like a mastermind help not only when business is up, but also when there are unpredictable challenges.

<u>TOOLS</u>

Chris Kelly:

Going into a general topic again, what tools should every entrepreneur have in order to get started, in order to get their name out there, and in order to just get attention in general?

Mitch Durfee:

Well, if you're talking about filling a funnel full of leads in your business, I would say social media is something that you can absolutely just crush. It is way too easy to add someone new to your network every single day. In fact, I encourage you to all reach out to just one new person a day. That's 365 more people you can add to your network every single year if you just add one new person a day. I remember when Facebook came out, I was in Iraq I thought, "That's stupid." Of course, I got a profile because if you had an army email address, you could get it.

Mitch Durfee:

I was in Iraq, and I signed up for it. I put my picture up there, and I had one picture. I remember I got my first few friend requests, and I'm like, "Oh, that's cool." Now if I knew the amount of power that I could have used 10 years ago with social media and LinkedIn and Instagram that I have today, I would be milestones ahead. Now I want to inspire you, if you have ever watched the ABCs or the NBCs or the TBS channels. With Social media you can take your initials, (for me MMD), and you own that TV broadcasting channel. Every single day, if I want to, I can broadcast my message. In a matter of seconds people can follow and share my message for me. If you have a business, or even as a professional social media is one of the tools that you have to use.

Chris Kelly: What about on the financial side? I know a couple real estate investors who track everything through Excel. I know a couple businesses who use QuickBooks. What would you recommend if you're just getting started, for the financial piece?

Mitch Durfee: Lets go back to the millionaire business mindset principle of building a team. Depending on what it is exactly that you are doing, your million dollar team, will have someone that should be able to solve that problem for you. For myself though I love using technology so quickbooks online is what I use. Find something that works for you, and stick with it.

Mitch Durfee:

Personally, I like anything in the cloud because I travel a lot, and I want to be able to access it. If I use a system or process like QuickBooks, or FreshBooks, or any of these bookkeeping softwares, I definitely want something that I can share with other people on my team. Today, I think it's important to realize if you're using technology ... Or if you're not using technology in your business, if you're using an Excel sheet on your computer, you have to figure out a way that you can make that manageable by other people, so your million dollar team can help you create your million dollar dream.

NEW CUSTOMERS

Chris Kelly: We've talked about social media, we've talked about financials. Obviously, you're a big proponent on creating websites. How do you get your website to attract attention and new customers?

Mitch Durfee: When it comes to websites, onlinestartupbox.com can build you the most beautiful website for your business. It's very easy to go out, and hire a web designer. The only trouble with a website is these days its like having the world's most perfect car for sale in the middle of the desert hidden behind a giant sign, if no-one see's it does it matter? Yes, it may matter to you, but are customers going to be attracted to it if they can't see it? You have to think about traffic when it comes to website design.

Mitch Durfee: You're one website in a sea of millions. How do you get your site in front of the right people? There's a lot of different techniques for that, and I think honestly the best way to do it, is to come down to creating value for other so other customers can start to refer you, share it, and create the content for you.

Mitch Durfee:

For example, we had a business reach out to us and they said, "I love your products. I would love to create a partnership for this how can we work together." We created an affiliate link for them. Through that affiliate link, they're able to promote our products for us, their customers get an exclusive offer, and they get paid a commision for selling our products.

Mitch Durfee:

Affiliate links is one way to generate traffic. Now before we go to far on generating traffic you must integrate some sort of lead follow-up system. As important as traffic is it does nothing if you are not capturing the leads. Spending money on pay-per-click traffic is the fastest way to get overnight traffic. You can send PPC traffic through different platforms like Facebook Ads, which we've mastered in our first business, and also Google Ads. With Goggle if you type in red, T-shirt, and certain town, you MUST show up for that term if that's your business. If you sell red T-shirts in, I don't know...

Chris Kelly: Kentucky.

Mitch Durfee: ... Kentucky. Red T-shirts in Kentucky, and you type that in and you don't show up, well your business is going to the person that has red T-shirts in Kentucky, whoever that may be.

Mitch Durfee: You have to understand that whatever business you are in, you have to show up in order for people to realize that you are the solution to their problem. As a real estate agent if people don't know that I'm a real estate agent, it is my fault! If I'm a real estate investor and I'm buying houses, and no one knows that I buy houses again my fault. What happens is the home owner ends up selling it to the person right in my backyard because they know about them. I must do my job as a business owner or a business entrepreneur to be first in mind.

Chris Kelly: It sounds like all businesses still rely on who you know, instead of what you know. Your net worth is directly correlated to your network.

Mitch Durfee: Yes. Your network is definitely correlated to your net worth. The five closest people you surround yourself with can be connected with your average income.

Mitch Durfee: I can tell you this, when I started adding amazing all-star players to my network, it opened up more opportunities. One of the best hires I've ever had was literally through asking someone, " I'm looking to hire people, who do you know?" When I sat down with that person, I didn't know at that time that he was gonna be such an amazing asset to our team. I didn't know what was in front of me. But it.was only because I knew the person before him that introduced me to him. Yes, every business that you're ever in, shake hands, introduce yourself, learn how you can help them.

Mitch Durfee: When it comes to networking, this is the part that I always want to address because it's annoying if you're only selling, but if you're providing value, it becomes worth it. For example, if you come to me and you say, "I sell a juice drink that makes you lose weight and gives you more energy, and you sleep better, and blah blah blah." I'm like, "That's great. But I don't care about losing weight, getting better sleep, or having more energy. I'm good where I'm at. I'm not a candle, I don't burn out."

Mitch Durfee: Don't sell me something I don't need, ask me questions first. Figure out how you can help me, and I'll ask the same. If you have a solution that resolves my challenges offer it, but more importantly I'll connect you with someone that needs more energy, wants to lose weight, or needs to sleep better. Don't go to your network and always be trying to sell them. Go to your network and provide value to them first and they will connect you with those who need your product or service.

Chris Kelly: Do you think that a business can survive today without a social media presence, without a financial system set up, without a decent website, without decent traffic being served or focus on their social media platforms?

Mitch Durfee: I think it's possible to survive, but it's not possible to thrive. What I mean by that is yes, you will always get by if you are just doing enough to get by. You'll always have the same challenges with mediocrity. If a competitor decides to come open shop next door, and you're a small mom-and-pop shop, you have no social media, you have no technology in place, and you have no systems, they will eat you alive!

Chris Kelly: How did you gain attention on social media? I know one of the things that I've seen that I particularly enjoy is the selfie challenges that you have done in the past.

Mitch Durfee: Earlier on we talked about Grant Cardone. He said, "Anytime you do something, you have to 10x it. You need people to know what you do." One of the biggest challenges of coming back from Afghanistan is not having a network at all, so people didn't really know who I was. I was a new face in a new town, even though I grew up here. In order for people to know more about me, and know more about what I offer, and know who I serve, I had to become recognizable.

Mitch Durfee: In order to do that, I started doing the selfie challenge. I literally started taking a selfie a day. I would take a selfie with every single person I'd bump up against. Even to this day, I still love taking selfies with people because 1) it introduces me to their network, so now their network knows who I am, and I introduce them to my network. I get to help them meet people every single day, and they get to help me meet new people that I can serve. The selfie challenge was probably simply, I would say, hands down, one of the best things that I ever did in my business.

Chris Kelly: Do you feel like it was successful because it was creative, because it was fun, because there was a low point of entry to where anybody could participate?

Mitch Durfee: Yeah. What made the selfie challenge so successful was that I could call anyone out, and have them drop their selfies.... People were always joking about taking selfies. Some people have a negative connotation with the selfie, and then

125

some people would just absolutely loved them. They thought it was hilarious.

Mitch Durfee: It was easy for me to do because it cost me nothing. It was gorilla marketing because I could reach so many. It was an opportunity that 1) I could literally do anywhere with every single person that I ever met. It was something that was completely organic, so it grew without actually trying. It was so easy. How fast as you can you take a selfie? Boom. How fast can you meet someone. Boom, that is quick marketing.

Chris Kelly: What about vlogging?

Mitch Durfee: Vlogging I've done a few times... To this day, I haven't had the results that I wanted to get from vlogging. My YouTube is getting subscribers, but it's not getting the results that I'm dreaming of. However, on Facebook, I am constantly battling up against that 5,000 friends, and I have to unfortunately remove friends or invite them to like my other business pages. Like "MitchDurfeeOfficial"

Mitch Durfee: Vlogging, if you tell the story right, people are interested in it. But no one cares if you wake up, eat Cheerios, jump on the bus, and you do nothing during the day. It's all about the story. If you're telling a story that relates to them, then it'll be a home run every single time. But if you're telling a story about your Cheerios, and how you walked the dog, you're not going viral anytime soon.

Chris Kelly: Something else that you do on a daily basis is you reach out to your friends, your business partners, in some manner. Sometimes it can even be as simple as asking a basic question, to where you get some community involvement. Is that important for staying in the forefront of everyone's mind?

Mitch Durfee: Yeah. I do it purposely and intentionally. I reach out to the closest people to me and inside my mastermind group 1) because I want to see if there's anything that I can do to help them bridge any kind of gap or hurdle that may have come up. Most times these phone calls are just little check-ins, "Hey, how are things? Hey, I was just thinking about you. Hey, I was listening to this idea and I wanted to share this concept with you."

Mitch Durfee: But yes to answer your question, in business, in sales, in everything that you do when it comes to that business millionaire mindset is you have to be in front of other peoples' minds so that they're think of you when they have a challenge that you offer a solution to. It's like follow-up. If you're in sales, you got to follow-up seven times before they think of you. In business, when you find these people that are providing amazing value to you, you have to stay in front of them as frequently as possible because that's the only way to organically grown the operations that you're focused on.

Chris Kelly: Another thing that you touched on is Facebook limits your audience to 5,000 people. How do you reach a larger audience beyond those 5,000?

Mitch Durfee: Reaching a larger audience isn't as important as having the right audience. When it comes down to building an audience for an entrepreneur. There are a couple reasons for it, one being if you have 100 people that are in your network, you could reach out to 100 people and you say, "Hey, I'll solve a problem for you for one-dollar." Even if every one of those people gave you a dollar, you would only make $100. If you have a megaphone of 5,000 people, and you say, "Hey, I have a solution to your problem and its only one-dollar." If 5,000 people all say yes, then you've made $5,000. That is a huge difference just because the size of your megaphone is larger. The bigger your network, the more problems you can solve, the more you impact the world and the more rewarded you are both financially and internally.

Mitch Durfee: To go back, yes, currently Facebook has shut people off at 5,000 people. I suggest pick one platform, dive as deep as you can into that platform. Once you've mastered that, then expand into other platforms. It only took me three months to get 5,000 followers on Instagram, because I already had a following on another channel.

Mitch Durfee: Instagram allows you to have a lot more. But again, dive deep on one. Right now, currently, Instagram is probably one of the fastest growing platforms. If you're not on Instagram, using it to the fullest extent at this time, then you're probably missing out on some opportunities, whether it's your business, you could get more sales, or it's your network and you can add more people into your circle of influence, you have to be using social media for that.

Chris Kelly: Do you utilize different social mediums for the different message that you're trying to deliver?

Mitch Durfee: I do...Unfortunately, with having all these different entrepreneurial industries, it does become a challenge because people recognize me for the guy that builds websites, has a real estate sales team, public speaker and trainer, online courses, business coaching, mastermind groups and retreats, author, real estate investor and a few others. If I did an update for each one of those things that I do every day on one single broadcast channel, my message would distract the end consumer. So I rarely promote my offers through my personal social profiles, I create groups and use paid advertising to put my specific message in front of the right audience for each "profession" I also want to say that as we are talking about this it sounds like a lot of things. The honest truth is, I've built a team of incredibly talented individuals that assist me with 90% of those tasks. My own personal million dollar team!

Mitch Durfee: On Facebook I create a new Page and Group for real estate investing, Real Estate Property Warriors because other people have similar goals with real estate investing they assit me in the management of the page. I personally selected those people to make sure their goals aligned with my vision for the group. Next I use ads or pay-per-click traffic, to target other people outside of my personal network. I'm not targeting my network with those ads because again, I don't want to clutter up the message to my personal network.

Chris Kelly: Going onto getting new customers and growing your business, so there's organic and there's not organic. I know we've talked about hitting social media. Are there any other methods that you use in order to get people organically?

Mitch Durfee: When it comes to customers, customers could care less about what you do, they're looking to solve a problem.

Mitch Durfee: Organically, yes, you will organically get customers, from time to time. You have to put your product in front of them before they actually know that they need your product. One of the things that we did in our businesses was we tied it to having a social cause. Our Grunts Move Junk mission was to put our vets back into the workforce. Our business became tied to the social cause of helping our veterans.

Mitch Durfee: You see a lot of these other businesses like " Hey, come rent a bicycle from us, and we'll donate $10 to the St. Jude's Fund." It's like, okay, that's a great company, but how does that align with your brand, your business, and the value that you're providing with your service? I'm not saying that St. Jude's Fund is a bad program, I'm just saying that you should align your message with your mission. For us, being that we were service members we loved serving our community. We did a lot of different community events and donated thousands of dollars over the years. When we're able to do community events around the veteran concept, it aligned with our brand and was able to drive a lot more interest in what we actually do. "I've heard about you guys before. What is it you do?" Our community service opened up the conversation when we were doing these events.

Mitch Durfee: Plus event marketing, you're getting out there in your community and you're doing more stuff for your community. That's ultimately the main purpose of a quality business is to provide a product or service that makes the community and world a better place.

Chris Kelly: You specifically put in your motto, "give back."

Mitch Durfee: Absolutely. Yeah, our mission was to help others. From the beginning, it was to place our veterans back into the workforce. That's what we did because at the end of the day, we're trying to help people. That's also why I wrote the book, Serve 2 Win, it was crafted purposely to help people become successful so they can help even more people.

BUILDING YOUR TEAM

Chris Kelly:

Getting back to the generality of excluding all of your Grunts experience, what would you look for, if you had to start all over, what would you look for in a new hire?

Mitch Durfee:

My "How to Build a Million Dollar Team" course covers this, When it comes to building a million dollar team, You're looking for the right person, I believe the biggest thing and the most important thing you could ever do when it comes to hiring a good team member is to interview as many people as possible.

Mitch Durfee:

For example, Imagine you had one diamond in front of you and had to pick the best diamond. By default you only have one option. Now imagine you had nine more diamonds in front of you. As you begin to look at these diamonds, That first diamond looked great all by its self but is it still the biggest, best, brightest, shiniest, clearest cut diamond? The same thing happens when you add the best diamon on the team. However, when you start to add diamond number two and diamond number three, diamond number one doesn't look as good anymore. Diamond number one's a little faded. Maybe it has a little crack down the center, or the cut's not as sharp as two and three.

Mitch Durfee: When you interview more people, for example, 10 different diamonds, you're able to pick the best one out of ten, which means that you actually have something to compare it to. When you're building a team, make sure you're testing it against others, because when you find a group of perfect diamonds that's when everything starts to come together.

Chris Kelly: With restaurants, with Grunts, with construction, they're really hard jobs. You're outside, it's hot. How do you entice the best talent when your market probably isn't the most ideal?

Mitch Durfee: You will realize over time that no matter what industry you're in, people rarely absolutely dream about going to work. They dream about going on vacation, the dream about the the pursuit of

135

happiness but they don't schedule it out on their calendar every day, "Yes, tomorrow I'm going to work." That's not their dream vision. However, when there is a purpose that they feel a part of, it is much easier to get them to enjoy what it is that they're doing. How do you entice the best talent to come into these industries? Well, it all comes down to the story and vision of the company.

Mitch Durfee: For example, if you're hiring people for a very physically demanding job, spin it and say, "You get to work out while you work." If you're hiring someone for a restaurant position and it's not, "You get to make food." It's, "Master the skills used by top leading chefs" You spin the job description to the new team members desired outcome. Also if your companies vision is to solve a similar problem they can relate to. The experience at work provides the result that they want outside of work. That's how you get the best talent to join your forces.

Chris Kelly: What methods have you used to actually motivate your employees?

Mitch Durfee: When it comes to motivation, I like to compare it with a sports analogy. You need a coach that comes in and he needs to motivate... The coach comes into the locker, and when he comes into the locker room, everyone's sitting there and they're waiting for him to say something that drives them forward. He has to rally them up, pump them up, and get them believing anything is possible and point them in the direction.

Mitch Durfee: That motivational speech, it may only last a day or two. It's not easy to do every single time, and it takes a lot of time and demand on the coach. Yes, sometimes you have to motivate to get over the goal line. However, what I found is if you get them to see and believe in the over all dream of the company it's much more easier to get them to do the long-term gains, versus the short term motivational success.

Chris Kelly: You've even gone into figuring out what motivates the individual because a lot of times it's not money, which is gonna make them work harder.

Mitch Durfee: Exactly where I'm going with this. When it comes to motivation, I think it's more important to lead. If you're leading the people on your team, you get much bigger results. How do you lead someone? It's not through motivation, it's more about learning what actually excites them.

Mitch Durfee: For example, some people love gifts. If I needed someone to stay a couple extra hours, and I knew that they liked gifts. I can bring them a gift and ask, " You don't have to do say yes, but if you would help me out," I'm able to get that result from them.

Mitch Durfee: Here's the big challenge though. If they don't like gifts and you give them a gift, you're gonna get the complete opposite reaction. "Oh, cool. You tried to bribe me with a gift." It doesn't work well when you use the wrong love language to communicate with a person.

Mitch Durfee: Some people just want recognition. Next time you're at a company meeting, pick out two or three people that really feed off of recognition and you say, "Hey, by the way, so and so did an incredible job. I just wanted to share that at the meeting. So and so, he or she did this_____. Without them we would be ____" At that same company meeting, if you give the gift to the person who loves gifts, then they're gonna glow.

Mitch Durfee: If you swap those two languages, and you give the recognition to the person that wants the gift, and the gift to the person that wants the recognition, you will not get the same results at all. It's important to learn what leads them so that you can get the desired results from them.

Chris Kelly: This is a very nuanced question, but how do you balance being a team member, being a leader, and being the driving force of a business? It's more important for the business as a whole, for you to create new leads, get new money, and push for new business as much as possible to keep everybody employed and busy.

Mitch Durfee: In business, it's critical to be focused on the two parts of every business. 1) the business that makes money today, and 2) the business that makes money tomorrow. What I mean is, when you have the million dollar team in place that can't handle any more new business that you bring in, your focus moves from generating business to supporting the team. If you see everyone digging through the piles of work with a metaphorical shovel and you begin shoveling, everyone else on that team will work harder.

Mitch Durfee: The will respect you more if they look over and see you, working hard to support them and they'll believe when there is to much work, we know that our leadership will support us in anyway possible. That is critical when you are building your team.

Mitch Durfee: The second part is you have to have the million dollar business mindset. You have to be focusing on what makes money in the future. That isn't always getting in the trenches. If I do have to get in the trenches for whatever reason, then I also have to put in more time understand what actions lead to my team not being able to handle the flow and to work with my team to create a new system when the same challenge comes up in the future. If I missed something that allows me to get into the trenches with the shovel, then I have to go back and I have to commit that time so that in the future, that doesn't happen again. Create a resource, or a system, or a process that's in place that allows me to have maintain that million dollar business mindset so that it's not me doing all of it.

Chris Kelly: Does the CEO always have to be the one that works the hardest?

Chris Kelly: Or put in the most hours, or come up with the best ideas? Because ultimately, you want to have the team to push your ideals forward. But initially are the CEOs, the ones that have to do the most work, put in the most hours, and sacrifice the most for their company?

Mitch Durfee: When you're the CEO of your business, it's almost like you never actually turn it off. Even after you sell the business, I think there's still a part of you that still goes back and says, "I want to make sure that my team is still successful." If you see a cliff ahead and the team is marching in that direction, you want to save those troops before they get to the edge of the cliff. Success is the CEO's duty.

Mitch Durfee: I'm not saying that you have to put in more hours or work harder. However, what I am saying is that if there is a challenge, it falls on you. Keep In mind that high level of accountability you hold yourself to. Also your board of directors or mastermind group that you have to answer to. Another fun exercise is to imagine you could duplicate yourself. Look back at what you were doing for tasks daily as the CEO, would you hire yourself or would you fire yourself? Remember, at the end of the day, the success of the company is your obligation.

Chris Kelly: Just to elaborate on that, if there are weak points which everybody naturally has, it's your responsibility to hire someone who is an advisor, or put somebody directly on your team who can compensate for your shortcomings.

Mitch Durfee: Here's the deal, for me personally, paperwork is not my strong suit. I'm a forward thinker. I like to shoot for the moon. I can recognize talent, but I also recognize that there are organizing paperwork and things that I'm just not amazing at.

Mitch Durfee: For me, that means if I'm gonna hire someone, my first hire better be somebody that's really good at paperwork. That way, I can be more of a strategist, and focus on making sure that they're we are finding the right people for the team.

Chris Kelly: You've talked about putting in the work, building your team, being the best version of you, having a vision. There's so much involved with being successful at a level of a millionaire business. How do you avoid burnout? What is the best advice that you could give to the mom-and-pop who are trying to expand, who are struggling, and they're just having issues getting over the hump, and just want to say, "Forget it," and give it up?

Mitch Durfee: I would say that everyone out there that has that millionaire business mindset deep down inside them, has to remember that it's not always easy, but it is always worth it. When you're struggling, realize that you're not alone. Other people have struggled before. Keep in mind that it is going to be difficult. There are gonna be challenges, there are gonna be headaches and hurdles, but there's also gonna be times that you're on top of the mountain, you're taking the vacations, you're spending your time with friends and family, that bills aren't an issue because you've perfected your systems, you've put technology in place, you've hired the right people, you've got your million dollar team. When you do all this stuff, that millionaire business that you've always had in the back of your mind, becomes not only possible but also a reality.

Mitch Durfee: How do you avoid burnout? Every time you face a challenge, realize that if that challenge was solved properly, would it still be a challenge? When you solve the problem, and yes there are tons of them, over time, those things create momentum behind you, because success builds on success.

Mitch Durfee: Yes, I would be lying if I said, "I don't ever get tired." Although, sometimes I'm

144

able put in some pretty decent amount of hours. On average, I like to start around 5 o'clock in the morning, and I usually end around 12:00-12:30 at night. I set my alarm but I'm often up and out of the bed before it goes off. I take a cold shower even in the winter, I eat my breakfast, and I'm out the door because I know that what I'm working on is much bigger than where I'm at currently. In order to do that, there are things that I have to accomplish.

Mitch Durfee: To be clear simply put, avoiding burnout comes down to making sure that you have a bigger purpose and a good healthy system. If your body is not healthy, then you won't have the energy to lead. You can't march to the top of the mountain if you don't have the physical body to be able to support this. That just means eating healthy, and staying hydrated. If you need a day off, know when you're at your limits, take that day off.

Mitch Durfee: I always like to say, "I'm not a candle. I don't burn out." I do get tired, but I just keep moving forward, I remember to breathe, I keep smiling, I keep my energy up, and I surround myself with people that when I have a challenge, I can pass the baton over to them.

Chris Kelly:

On that positive note, I can't think of a better way to wrap up this book. Where can they reach out to you if they have any questions or want any further advice?

Mitch Durfee:

Thank you for following The millionaire business mindset, remember you truly are amazing, so surround yourself with amazing people. You can connect with me at mitchdurfee.com and follow me on social media @mitchdurfee. If you haven't already, go to amazon or serve2win.com to pick up a copy of my #1 Best selling book Serve 2 Win. Also check out How to Build a Million Dollar Team, so you can free up more of your time and create generational wealth. Lastly always remember progress is more important then perfection, I believe in you!

CPSIA information can be obtained
at www.ICGtesting.com
Printed in the USA
LVHW050417040520
654931LV00007B/1849